the five levels *of* pleasure

the five levels *of* pleasure

Enlightened Decision Making for Success in Life

NOAH WEINBERG

"There is ultimately only one motivating factor in all decision making: pleasure." –*Noah Weinberg*

SelectBooks, Inc.
New York

The Five Levels of Pleasure: Enlightened Decision Making for Success in Life

This edition published by SelectBooks, Inc.
For information address SelectBooks, Inc., New York, New York.

First Edition

ISBN 978-1-59079-123-3

Library of Congress Cataloging-in-Publication Data

Weinberg, Noah.
 The five levels of pleasure : enlightened decision making for success
in life / Noah Weinberg. -- 1st ed.
   p. cm.
 Includes bibliographical references and index.
 ISBN 978-1-59079-123-3 (pbk. : alk. paper)
 1. Success. 2. Pleasure. 3. Decision making. I. Title.

BJ1611.2.W398 2008
170'.44--dc22

2007047688

Manufactured in the United States of America

10 9 8 7 6 5 4 3 2 1

"Noah Weinberg is a wonderful teacher who has made it his mission to address the significant life issues that every person faces every day. He explores the wisdom and relevancy of informed, ethical decision-making with the goal of enabling every person to attain his or her full potential. Thank you for the good work you do and the message you put out. You have made a great difference in my life."—*Joseph Bijou*

about the author

Noah Weinberg is a pioneering educator whose teachings emphasize maximizing true pleasure and success through meaningful activities.

He is the internationally acclaimed founder and Dean of Aish HaTorah College of Jewish Studies in Jerusalem and Aish International, a system of 35 outreach branches located on five continents in 25 major cities, with hundreds of thousands of members.

Weinberg completed his undergraduate studies at Johns Hopkins University, post-graduate studies at Loyola Graduate School and rabbinical ordination at Ner Yisroel Rabbinical College in Baltimore, Maryland. Weinberg established Aish HaTorah in 1974, and the organization has since grown exponentially, due to his inclusive world view and his exceptional communications and organizational skills. His tape series, "48 Ways to Wisdom," is popular throughout the world.

The author would like to thank the following people, without whom this book would not have come to fruition: Laszlo Nadler, who hatched the idea originally; David Dweck and Michael Roney, who have worked tirelessly on the project for many months; Yitzchak Freundlich, whose support was essential to making this book happen; as well as Kenzi Sugihara and his superb staff at SelectBooks.

contents

preface

We're pleasure seekers.

There are six billion human beings in this world. Every one of them is feverishly working away, 24/7/365, and as long as they live, they will be seeking pleasure.

When they get out of bed, it's because they think that they will have more pleasure on their feet than under the covers. Otherwise, they'd all hug their pillows.

Anybody who is aware realizes that this world is gorgeous, at least where humankind hasn't messed it up. Everybody knows that life is beautiful, and is seeking to enjoy it.

So how come there's so much misery, depression, violence and hate in a world of such pleasure? It's because people don't know how to get that pleasure.

> To see the truth in this, consider this: If someone won a lottery ticket and received $100 million after taxes, would they jump for joy? Of course.
>
> You might ask this person "What are you so excited about?" and he or she might say "Are you kidding? I can do anything I want!"
>
> So you come back 10 years later and now the person has $110 million, but he is miserable. You ask why and he says "Because I don't know what I want. And the few things that I do know I want, I can't get them. I want my wife to be happy. I'd like my children to be healthy, off drugs and hard working, and I don't know how to get that."

Money just won't get it done. Like this person, you need to find out how to reach your goals with what you already possess. A little self-examination can be a powerful thing in this situation, for once you reach a true understanding of what makes you tick, your possibilities for achievement and true happiness are unlimited.

So what are the keys to understanding yourself? You've got to start by knowing that you are the sole decision maker for your life. You can't live with other people's decisions. You've got to decide for yourself who you are and what you know about whatever it is that you're going to make a decision about.

The second thing that you've got to understand is what you are living for. What is available? You want something positive out of life. You're not living to be miserable, so what will make you happy?

Then, once you know what you're living for, how in the world do you attain it?

Here's the simple answer: You've got to use your head. The mind is a fantastic computer and a powerful instrument, and if you know what you're going for, and you're using clear, provable *definitions* of the concepts and events that surround you, then you'll succeed. You'll be confident in your beliefs and defend your decisions, unhindered by doubt, and unleashed to do all of which you are capable.

And that's why I decided to write this book. I wanted to put all of these concepts together in order to give you a practical roadmap that you can use to reach your full potential as a human, and achieve the highest level of happiness in your life. The way I see it, if you have that power, that *capability*, then you'll be able to use it not only for your own good, but also your family and for the betterment of humankind.

Your Journey Through the Book

I adapted this roadmap from a highly successful course that has enormously enriched thousands of lives, including those of students, internationally acclaimed artists, successful business people, and everyone in between. So now it's your turn!

No matter what your culture or religion is, the discussions in these pages will take you on a journey of self-examination, enlightenment, and empowerment, showing you how to profoundly change and shape your life to attain maximum satisfaction. Each section clearly defines a concept and shows how it applies to everyday life. Successive sections build upon previous understandings. The end result is self-mastery and growth toward ultimate happiness.

All you need to do is to take the time to read through each of these chapters consecutively. Stop to consider the exercises scattered throughout the pages and you'll be amazed at how your view of the world grows clearer and more useful.

I also strongly recommend that you take some time between chapters to delve a little deeper into the concepts we examine. You can do that with the suggested readings listed by chapter in the Appendix in the back of the book.

Be aware that no major point developed in this book should be wholly novel in concept. To the contrary, as a thinking human being, you are likely to have considered much, if not all, of the points presented at one time or another in your own personal growth and development. Consequently, each one should strike you as a self-evident truth. However, when each individual point is viewed as part of an integrated whole, and thought through in this manner, the totality of the picture that emerges will lead to a profound shift in the way you will view reality and live your life.

the five levels *of* pleasure

introduction

How many people can honestly say that they are completely satisfied with what life has to offer? How many can say, "Life's great"? How many truly feel that life is giving them everything they want and more?

Unfortunately, not many.

Most people are suffering, consciously or not, because they feel they are not using their full potential.

Go ahead and check that out. Ask yourself, ask your friends.

Studies have shown that human beings are using only 5% of their potential. If they use another 2%, they are super-achievers. That means *you* are probably wasting 95% of your potential, and that is tragic. No wonder you're dissatisfied!

One of the reasons that people don't use their potential is because they are afraid of the *pain* of change and the *frustration* of making efforts that don't succeed.

The simple solution lies in recognizing and achieving *true pleasure*, which everyone craves, but can be elusive if you don't understand what it is and how to recognize it.

No Pain, No Pleasure

Here's something to consider: Pain is really the price we must pay for pleasure. No pain, no pleasure.

Did you ever go to a store and pay good money for a package of frustration? Everyone has. For example, let's say you buy a 1,000-piece jigsaw puzzle and go home looking to spend a Sunday assembling it. What if you opened the box and noticed that each piece was numbered according to where it fit in the puzzle. Just connect 1 to 2, 2 to 3...You'd be outraged! You'd go back to the store and say, "give me my money back" and the manager might respond, "We just wanted to make it easier for you." Without the challenge—yes, the *frustration* of putting the puzzle together—you don't have any fun.

The pursuit of pain and frustration is even a way of life for many who are seeking to reach their full potential. Take yoga, for example. There are several types of yoga, but some of them are actually based on a level of pain and frustration.

"Pain" yoga is exemplified by those fellows who sleep on a bed of nails. The idea is that if you can accept pain you can handle anything, and you feel released. But it's really about much more than simply accepting physical pain. It's about accepting the pain of failure, of being insulted, of controlling your temper.

Then there is "frustration" yoga: the guys who sit on the flagpole, who don't move while the flies walk up and down their noses. Can you imagine!? Now that's accepting frustration. The idea behind this practice is to become the master of your body, but it is also about dealing with many other kinds of frustrations: the frustration of trying to understand the unknown; of the choices you have made in life; of finding solutions.

Pain and frustration. It doesn't sound like very much fun, but every pleasure in life has a price tag attached to it. This price tag is effort.

Moreover, the greater the pleasure, the greater the price, the greater the effort needed to acquire it. Superficial pleasures require far less effort to attain. The effort involved in winning a game of tic-tac-toe is nothing like the effort involved in winning a marathon, and there is no comparison between the pleasure that each of the victors receives.

However, to truly appreciate any pleasure, you must focus on that pleasure and not on the price tag associated with it. If you focus on the pleasure, you will not notice the effort; but if you focus on the effort, you will not notice the pleasure.

The Five Levels of Pleasure

With this book you'll learn about these higher levels of pleasure and how to attain them in order to achieve complete happiness and personal empowerment. You'll also learn that each higher level of pleasure is qualitatively magnitudes above the one before it. A million units of fifth class pleasure cannot acquire a single unit of fourth-class pleasure, and no amount of fourth-class pleasure can acquire a unit of third class pleasure, and so on. Each successive level is so qualitatively superior to the previous level that it is non-exchangeable.

Moving up the pleasure ladder is worth the effort. And if you do the work, you life will be infinitely more fulfilled.

✳ **FIFTH CLASS PLEASURE: Physical Pleasure**
This is the most common form of pleasure, and the one that often comes to mind for most people. When you enjoy a fine meal at a gourmet restaurant, or perhaps lounging on your couch watching a good movie, you're enjoying Fifth Class Pleasure. This class includes anything that involves the "five senses."

✳ **FOURTH CLASS PLEASURE: Love**
Everyone knows and understands the beautiful pleasure of love. Love is qualitatively more pleasurable then all physical pleasures combined, and is worth more than all the money in the world. Yet real love takes work and commitment. If you want that pleasure, it is available in every relationship. You just have to be willing to pay the price.

✳ **THIRD CLASS PLEASURE: Conviction**
As powerful as love is, it's trumped by the drive for *conviction*, the will to do the right thing according to one's values, and events in the world prove it every day. All the love in the world and all the money in the world are not worth one moment of this third class pleasure.

✳ **SECOND CLASS PLEASURE: Creativity**
The positive expression of power—to affect the world in some way—is creativity, and the true source of creative power is wisdom. In order to create you must first formulate a concept in your mind that you desire to translate into reality.

✳ **FIRST CLASS PLEASURE: Ultimate Meaning**
This is sensing the interconnectedness of existence and one's place in the infinite scheme of reality (the transcendental experience).

It's All About Decision Making

Ultimately, the achievement of these higher levels of pleasure is all about making the right decisions. And let's face it: in choosing between all options in life, we chose the one we think will give us the most pleasure. Obviously, as we mature, we come to realize that sometimes we must forego short-term pleasures and quick fixes for deeper, and more meaningful, experiences. In the end, however, underlying it all is this pleasure principle.

> When you woke up this morning, you made a decision: Get out of bed or stay in bed. How did you decide? Somewhere in the deep recesses of your sleepy head, you asked yourself: "Is it worth it? Should I stay in the cozy, warm, comfortable bed, or should I make the effort to get up now and be on time for class (or work)?" Here you had a choice: Sleep or get up on time. On what basis did you decide? What factors were important? Was it not a choice between which option would give you the greatest level of pleasure? If there had been no downside to staying in bed, then that would have been a very pleasurable option. If, on the other hand, your grade or your job had been at risk by coming late, then making the effort to be on time would have provided the greater pleasure.

Even when we do something altruistic, we do it because it gives us pleasure.

> You are walking down the street, and a homeless person asks you for money. The crucial issue is whether you get more pleasure by keeping your spare change for whatever it will buy you, or is the satisfaction of helping the poor fellow out worth more to you? Is there another motivation at work here? (If you decide not to give based on a belief that the money will only be used on alcohol or drugs, are you not making a decision because of the satisfaction that you are getting out of knowing that you have done the right thing?)

It's clear: Every decision a human being makes in life has the same final criterion: "Will it give me pleasure or not?" That is the constant, whether the decision is something relatively trivial, such as what to have for dinner or what to do with your spare time, or whether it is something important such as whom to marry or what career to choose. Pleasure is the defining criterion.

A World of Possibilities

The five classes of pleasure are interdependent. Each builds on the other, and each level is necessary.

The bottom line is that we live in a world filled with possibilities. This world offers an entire spectrum of pleasures. We have to be conscious of what is available and learn to direct at least part of our efforts higher up on the scale. Each successive class of pleasure requires a greater level of effort to achieve.

Just as when you enjoy a good glass of wine, you need to become a connoisseur of those higher classes of pleasure in order to recognize and appreciate them. And once you get a taste, the world opens up to you and there's no going back.

Let's get started....

chapter 1

the ABCs *of* Life

Most people are fixated on physical, material pleasure.

This kind of pleasure is wonderful, but it doesn't create happiness. Someone can have a hundred million dollars, all of the toys and luxuries known to humankind, a beautiful and intelligent mate, and still be miserable, or perhaps just not satisfied with life.

So what is the way out of that misery? The key is in finding higher pleasures; the pleasures people never tire of.

Achieving these higher pleasures requires a clear-minded, informed effort on your part. And it *does* take effort. After all, we all accept the maxims that "there's no free lunch," and "no pain, no gain." (Choose your metaphor.)

Yet the effort required to experience these pleasures is most definitely worth every ounce of energy you invest! And this incredibly fulfilling journey begins with identifying a set of fundamental principles.

Think about it: Every system in existence has its basic fundamental principles—building blocks without which you cannot proceed.

* In art, you have to learn how to draw in proportion and how to mix colors.

* In medicine, you have to learn anatomy and physiology before you can proceed to diagnostics and treatment techniques.

* In mathematics, you must learn how to add, subtract, multiply and divide before proceeding to the more advanced fields of algebra and calculus.

* In music, you learn about notes, time signatures and keys before being able to compose complex pieces.

Life, too, has its basics, its ABCs, its foundation upon which all else is built. This is true regardless of your gender, religion, or ethnic background.

We are all physically, genetically, and spiritually, human beings. Although our cultural backgrounds may vary, we are more similar than different. With this in mind, reason argues that in the fields of decision-making, practical ethics, *and yes, even human happiness,* the building blocks of a fulfilled life are consistent among us.

Just as art, medicine, mathematics, and music are each universal languages with consistent universal principles, so too the fundamentals of a happy life must likewise be universal.

Consider this analogy: Houses are built in many different styles of architecture; they may be built in different shapes, painted in different colors, and roofed in different materials. Yet, all houses are built on a basic foundation, poured from concrete, making them strong and stable. What is built on top of that foundation is mostly a matter of taste. Similarly, human happiness is built on a foundation of fundamental, shared, human principles. To succeed at the art of living, then, these need to be understood. In terms of human interaction, our individuality is a function of our personalities, unique family, and cultural background. Nevertheless, these details of our lives are like the features of a home—the style and coloring are our own, but they are all erected on a shared type of foundation.

This chapter will show you how to identify these basic fundamentals of decision-making.

Exercises ~

❶ Do you agree with the notion that certain universal principles underlie every individual's ability to live a happy life? Do you agree with the notion that certain universal principles guide ethical decision-making— that these principles cross national and cultural barriers? Why or why not?

❷ Try to list five basic principles that are absolute prerequisites to living a happy life. Try to list five basic principles that are absolute prerequisites to living an ethical life. Try to list five basic principles that are absolute prerequisites to effective decision-making.

The "A" of Life:
Assumptions Can't Be Accepted Blindly

How do you know right from wrong? How are you able to distinguish truth from falsity?

We live in a complex and rapidly changing world. Every day we are inundated with ideas and opinions from our friends, family, teachers, and supervisors, as well as from a plethora of entertainment and advertising media. With so much information directed at us, much of which is misinformation, how do we figure out who is right and who is wrong, who is telling the truth and who is lying?

The "A" of life is all about *analyzing* how information is conveyed to us, when it is accepted as true, and how our *acceptance* of information determines the basis of our knowledge and beliefs.

Would you agree that most people generally accept as true what they are taught?

We are all creatures of our society, and every society holds certain values and beliefs about life. The sum total of these beliefs becomes the consciousness unique to that society. We absorb that consciousness through what we are taught at home and in school, through the books we read, and through the movies we watch. For the most part, our society has created for each of us a "default philosophy" of how we view the world.

This raises some interesting questions:

* Since we are so profoundly influenced by our societies, how do we discern our own independent beliefs and identity?

* Is it even possible for us to come to any truly independent conclusions about the world around us?

* Is it even possible for us on our own to distinguish between right and wrong, or are we condemned to being mere moral automatons programmed by our society?

To illustrate the difficulty of these questions, consider whether an 18-year-old German in 1939 was morally responsible for voluntarily choosing to join the SS and committing the atrocities associated with that military unit.

While pondering this issue, also consider the relevance of a famous and chilling experiment conducted at Yale University some years ago by Dr. Stanley Milgram.[1]

> Dr. Milgram told subjects that they would be participating in a study to determine how punishment affects a person's ability to learn. The subjects were introduced to a man who, they were told, was the subject of the experiment and who would attempt to memorize a list of words (this man was in fact Dr. Milgram's collaborator in the experiment).
>
> Every time this man would make a mistake in memorization, the real subjects of the experiment would be asked to push a button giving increasingly strong electric shocks to the man memorizing words (in fact, of course, no shock was actually given as the man supposedly memorizing words was an actor collaborating with the real experiment taking place).
>
> Each time the experiment would begin, the real subjects would nervously laugh as they heard grunts of acted-out pain, supposedly provoked by the initial electric shocks. As the dosage appeared to increase, screams would emanate from the adjacent room. The experiment administer would then appear in a white lab coat to encourage the subjects to continue providing shocks.

[1] See *Suggested Reading* number five.

Meanwhile the collaborator would plead to stop the experiment, saying that it was hazardous to his heart. The experiment showed that the great majority of subjects continued to give electric shocks to the point where they believed that they had nearly killed the collaborator.

In other words, even where the subjects' own senses told them that they were physically harming another person by administering high voltage electric shocks, the instructions of an "authority" figure continued to be obeyed. The experiment documented that there is instinctive reaction to trust authority figures rather than question them.

By implication, the experiment also demonstrates that you do not have to be evil or sadistic to put people into gas chambers, to be involved in ethnic cleansing, or to shoot at civilians as a soldier. You only have to be completely normal—just not independent enough to ask whether or not what you are doing is moral.

Informed Decision Making: Figuring Out What You Believe

Unless you examine what you believe and why you believe it, it will be an accident of birth and surrounding culture whether you turn out to be a good or an evil person. Without such an examination, you are just part of the masses; your opinions and beliefs are not truly yours. As an individual, you do not really exist.

This understanding of what you believe, *and why*, is the key to informed decision-making, which in turn is the key to total self-fulfillment and accessing those higher levels of pleasure.

First and foremost, informed decision-making requires us, in a sense, to step outside ourselves and to judge whether our actions are indeed moral. Otherwise, the Nazi, the terrorist, the ethnic cleanser, the murderer, and the thief are all just products of their environment, their upbringing, and their culture. We can only say that people are morally accountable, once we say that it is possible for them to make an independent judgment about the correctness or incorrectness, the morality or immorality, of their actions.

> The concept of informed decision-making only begins when we say that some standard of behavior exists out there transcends the present situation, and we say that perceiving this transcendent reality is always possible.

This then is the challenge for each one of us: To actualize our potential as human beings, each of us must sort through the ideas and values that are promulgated to us, and then decide which are valid and which are not. Then, we must develop the intellectual and moral courage to live by what we have discerned as true, even if the whole world seems to stand opposed to us. Without engaging in such a process, we are nothing more than submissive products of our society—we are just one of the herd.

The "A" of life is that people acquire knowledge and beliefs to the extent that they accept information conveyed to them as being true, and this knowledge and these beliefs determine who we are and how we behave.

Therefore, *we all are responsible for critically analyzing information obtained*. The first step to becoming self-fulfilled and totally happy is to investigate and judge the validity of the assumptions underlying our actions.

Exercises ~

❶ A young Chinese man is drafted into the Army. Like most good citizens he loves his country and is now proud to wear its uniform. He wants to be a good soldier for the sake of his country, for the honor it brings to his family, and for his own personal success and future. This young man is now sent to Tiananmen Square where he is confronted with mobs of students threatening his country, but yet, they are his fellow citizens. His commanders have ordered the soldiers that if the students attempt to break through their ranks, they are to open fire. If the students charge his position, should this young soldier open fire or not? Consider the fact that if the students were to do so, they would clearly be breaking the law. Furthermore, if the young soldier does not follow orders, he will face a court martial, which will bring dishonor to his family, result in his imprisonment, and likely condemn him to a very bleak future.

❷ Who is the more moral person? The draft-dodging hippy in 1969 who flees to Canada upon receiving his draft notice? The son of the influential businessman who uses his father's contacts to get the "safe" military position of Army correspondent? The helicopter pilot who drops napalm in enemy territory, where civilians are likely to live?

❸ Do you intend to give your children the same type of religious upbringing that your parents gave you? Why?

❹ At the turn of the century, if a couple wanted to take a stroll along the beach, the man would likely be wearing a coat, tie, and hat, and the woman a long dress. Everyone else would more or less be dressed the same. Today, the couple is likely to be wearing shorts and T-shirts, and others might be wearing much less. What changed and is this a good thing?

❺ Do you think that the war crimes trials that took place in The Hague for actions by soldiers during the war in the Balkans were morally correct? Why? Is it morally just for civilians from countries not affected by war to judge actions taken by soldiers, when these civilians neither know the stress of war nor understand the deeply rooted social-historical-religious consciousness of the combatants? Isn't this one culture imposing its values on another?

❻ Is it intolerant to believe that you are right, that everyone else is wrong, and to try to convince them of the correctness of your opinion?

The "B" of Life: Behavior is Motivated by the Quest for Pleasure

Thus far we have determined that the "A" of life is the responsibility for knowing the correctness of the assumptions guiding your decision-making. These assumptions are the building blocks of your decision-making. They provide the framework, the perspective, within which you operate. Change the perspective, and a whole new world of options materializes. Your range of available choices shifts.

The "B" of life determines which of these options you will now choose.

The "B" of life is the primary motivating force behind all of our decisions. Given a set of options, the "B" of life is that factor responsible for determining our response. It drives a person and guides them through life. Awareness of its existence is therefore a powerful tool in understanding all behavior, and ethical behavior in particular.

To discover this force consider the following question:

What do parents want most for their children? Most parents answer: Their happiness!

When their children are happy and enjoying themselves, parents are energized. When their children are sad, parents get distracted. When their children are miserable, parents go out of their wits. Every two-year-old knows this. What do all children do, the world over, when they want something? They cry. Ever wonder why? Because it works! Parents cannot bear the tears, to see their children unhappy, so they give in.

Now imagine a child having fun playing a video game. This would give most parents satisfaction—especially if the parents had just purchased the game for the child as a Christmas or birthday gift. But what would happen when that same child becomes obsessed with the game and begins to play with it 16 hours a day? How would the parents feel then? Obviously, they would be concerned and frustrated. Parents want their children to play outside as well as indoors with video games. They want their children to expand their horizons to include many interests.

So it is not *simple happiness* that parents want for their children. Parents want something more. They want their children to have a more complete and deeper type of happiness. Parents want their children to have full lives, filled with a range of experiences.

And there's more. When the parents in our story attempt to coax their child to get some fresh air, they must necessarily employ an educational process that conveys this message to their child: that playing outside is more deeply satisfying.

To achieve this and to motivate the child, our parents have two options. First, they can positively intervene by attempting to show the child that it is in his or her best interest to go outside—that playing outside will give the child more pleasure than remaining glued to the video machine. Alternatively, the parents can punish the child or take away the game, in essence causing the child some level of pain, if the child refuses to give up the toy. This would be a negative form of intervention, but it reaches the same end. The parents create a situation where going outside to play becomes the more pleasurable experience.

Ultimately, what parents want for their children, what in the end motivates children, *and* what indeed is the primary motivation for all of us—is pleasure.

> **Whatever we do in life is based on our evaluation of whether an activity will give personal pleasure.**

Check Out The Evidence!

I just told you that the pursuit of pleasure motivates all of our actions. Is this true? Having been presented with this view, you have a responsibility to check it out. Don't just accept or reject this premise on face value. Think about it! Does it make sense? Examine the evidence!

Take a look at yourself and at others around you. Is there any other motivating force in life? Or, it is true that all decision-making, the basis of everything you do or could ever imagine doing, comes down to an evaluation of how much pleasure you will get out of the experience? If you disagree, you must ask yourself why. What evidence do you have to the contrary? What possible alternative can you offer? Is there something else? Is there a greater motivating force than pleasure?

Time Out: How Do We Define Pleasure?

Before we go any further, you should understand that there is some confusion in the field of philosophy when it comes to talking about such things as pleasure, happiness, and self-interest, as well as an inconsistency in the use of these terms among various experts.

There are two areas of philosophy to which this discussion belongs: *egoism* and *hedonism*.

There are two types of egoism. One is psychological egoism, which asserts that people are primarily *motivated* by self-interest. This is not what we're talking about here.

The second is "ethical egoism," which defines *morality* in terms of self-interest. This is also not what we're talking about, as we're speaking solely of human motivation, without passing any kind of judgment on the morality of this condition. Although pleasure is asserted to be the primary motivating force in the human condition, we haven't yet discussed the *moral* implications of this fact. (We're saving the good stuff for later!)

In the realm of philosophy relating to psychological egoism, three terms are generally misused. These are: Pleasure, happiness, and self-interest. *Webster*[2] defines these words as follows:

* ✳ *Pleasure* is a particular desire or purpose, a state or *condition of gratification of the senses* or mind.

* ✳ *Happiness* is a *state* of well-being … [an] *agreeable emotion* ranging in value from mere contentment to deep and intense joy in living.

* ✳ *Self-interest* is *one's own* interest or advantage.

Happiness is a *state of being*, whereas pleasure is a *sensation*. A pleasurable experience may lead you to being happy; but it could also leave you depressed (for example, people often feel guilty after engaging in morally-questionable, yet pleasurable, experiences, such as someone having an extramarital affair). Furthermore, you can be happy and experience pleasure, and you also can be depressed and still experience something pleasurable. Still, there is a connection between the two concepts: The level of pleasure that a happy person experiences from a pleasurable event, such as eating ice cream, is likely to be far greater than that of a depressed person.

Similarly, *pleasure* and *self-interest* are not synonymous. You can experience pleasure by helping other people, even though doing so might be considered against your "interest." For example, giving to charity could be considered against your interest since it results in a total loss of the amount given, though the experience is pleasurable as long as you are altruistically minded. Conversely, an activity that's in your interest, might prove to be non-pleasurable. For example, earning money at another's expense might ultimately leave you feeling miserable; yet engaging in such that act could be seen as being to your "advantage.

> Therefore, as we're defining it here, pleasure is the driving force of a person's decision-making, not happiness and not self-interest. We'll get deeper into the relationship between all of these forces later in the book.

---

[2] *Webster's Third New International Dictionary*. Meriam-Webster, Inc. (Springfield, 1993). [emphasis added]

Now let's look briefly at *hedonism*, another problematic area of philosophy when you're talking about the pursuit of pleasure, as we are. Hedonism comes in two types: *psychological* and *ethical*. To the decree that psychological hedonism encompasses the idea that all human behavior is motivated by the drive for pleasure, the ideas in this lesson, and indeed much of this book, could be called hedonistic. However, our view of pleasure is highly sophisticated and to a large degree inconsistent with the views of many hedonists. Likewise, the relationship we describe between pain and pleasure also contradicts much hedonistic philosophy.

Ethical hedonism is essentially a philosophy that defines good and evil in terms of pain and pleasure. Our present discussion relates specifically to motivation apart from moral judgments. Therefore, the concept of morality implied by hedonism is not the topic at hand.

Nonetheless, it is appropriate to point out at this point that, as we'll discuss in great detail later in the book, such a philosophy is based on a distorted understanding of the nature of, and relationship between, pain and pleasure.

Some hedonists reduce pleasure to being the only good end and assert that the self is a mere means for producing this end. Such a concept certainly opposes the philosophy presented here.

Exercises ~

❶ You hate pecans. Your spouse/significant other, however, loves pecan pie. For his or her birthday, you bake a pecan pie obviously with no desire to have any of it yourself. What is your primary motivation in baking this pie? Is your action purely *altruistic*, driven by a desire to please the person that you love? Or, is your motivation the deep sense of *personal satisfaction that you will receive* from knowing that you have pleased your loved one and from deepening bond of your relationship?

❷ You are the President of the United States. You have devised a plan to overhaul the American educational system in a way that you believe will increase standardized test scores and produce better citizenship. The only problem is that the opposing party controls Congress. What steps would you take to get a bill passed to implement your plan?

❸ You are a plastic surgeon. Your practice is fine, but your investments have all gone sour and now your home is threatened with foreclosure. A beautiful young woman comes into your office. She is obviously very wealthy (diamond earrings, designer clothes, and you see her Jag through your office window). She says that she wants you to reduce the size of her nose, which she has always regarded as too big. Looking at her, you do not have any clue as to why she would feel that way—she could be a model. You tell her that her nose looks fine to you, but she is insistent. Do you take the job?

The "C" of Life: Choosing the Correct Path is the Key to Pleasure

If we are right that the primary motivation of all action is the quest for pleasure, then it is logical that when you find yourself to be unhappy or frustrated, it must mean that you have made a mistake in your decision-making with regard to what will bring you the greatest level of pleasure. Does this make sense?

This is the "C" of life: People in general are not bad; they are mistake-prone. The chief reason we do not always get the pleasure we want, that we are unhappy, or that we have done things that we regret, is that we are constantly making mistakes—errors in judgment—as to what will bring us pleasure.

While we are active in the world, learning, doing, and going about our business, we are faced with a constant stream of choices, that lead us down various paths. Frequently, we choose poorly, thinking that one path will lead to the greatest level of pleasure, when in fact another direction would have brought us greater fulfillment.

Deep down, everybody wants to be good and to feel good. Everyone wants to fulfill his or her potential. But, we often think we can get that same pleasure by taking short cuts or choosing the easy way.

We want to have happy and fulfilled marriages, but we are unwilling to work at keeping our love for our spouses alive. We put other things in front of the necessary time investment required for a thriving family life. We pursue financial success and neglect other values, which may be more deeply satisfying. We want our lives to be personally meaningful, but we are swayed to act by social pressure.

All human beings want pleasure, but we make mistakes. These mistakes are the cause of our problems.

> In the book *The Seven Habits of Highly Effective People*,[3] Steven Covey tells the story of a man who approaches him for advice on how to rectify his failing marriage. The man tells Mr. Covey that he has fallen out of love with his wife. To this, Mr. Covey responds simply, "love her." The man, not understanding the message, persists with his description of the problem, to which Mr. Covey responds again, "love her." The man simply stares back. He fails to recognize that he has a choice. He can choose to walk down a path that will lead to divorce, because of a mistaken notion that perhaps he will be happier with a different wife, a different home, a different set of friends, and all the changes that accompany such a path. Or, he can chose to invest further in the relationship by giving to his wife and by engaging in the hard work that a marriage demands, and which in the end achieves the goal of forming that deep bond between two people that we call love.

---

[3] Covey, Stephen R. *The Seven Habits of Highly Effecive People: Powerful Lessons in Personal Change*. Simon & Schuster (New York, 1990). pp. 79-80.

Our lives are full of mistakes. In interpersonal relationships, some-times, we want to make ourselves feel better by hurting others who have hurt us. We put effort into getting even. In the end, though, we generally accomplish nothing and feel worse. How many times have we lashed out with a verbal assault, or nasty letter, directed at some-one who insulted us? What did this accomplish? For sure, it satisfies our immediate need for self-gratification, but did the action really redress the harm done? Did it repair the tear in the relationship that it was responding to?

Sometimes our mistakes have devastating circumstances, as shown in the story of Steve Brown (a real person, but not his real name).

> Mr. Brown was at the height of his life—married, children, great job, great friends, a BMW and more. One night, however, he decided to have a few too many beers, and then he decided to get into his car. He also decided to take along an old friend, but his friend never made it home. Mr. Brown was sentenced to 4 to 8 years in prison, and according to his lawyers he was lucky. They had expected 8 to 16. Now Mr. Brown has lost his job, his family, and his friends. He was an ordinary man, no different from many of us and no different from President of the United States George W. Bush, who was also arrested once for a DWI. But, Mr. Brown will not be running for president, and neither will he be spending the rest of his life with his sweetheart from college who divorced him, nor with his children who will be raised by a stepfather. Is he an evil man? What distinguishes him from Bush? Is it only that his luck ran out a little sooner?

Mr. Brown made a mistake in judgment. Perhaps it is unfair, but in the end, people are generally judged only in accordance with results. Therefore, Mr. Brown must live with the terrible consequences of his choice, while President Bush was little affected by his. In truth, though, everyone who drinks and drives, or who accompanies a drunken driver, makes the same mistake, thinking that the pleasure of getting to their destination faster and on their own, with all the attendant risks, is worth more than the inconvenience of finding alternative transportation. The only difference is the degree to which society holds them accountable.

Generally, our mistakes are not laden with such tremendous consequences. Although many of us have probably faced choices similar to Mr. Brown's, and maybe even made the same choice, our everyday choices are likely to be less dramatic. Yet, from the perspective of our own lives, all of our decisions have significant impact.

Did you ever have a day when nothing seemed to be going right? Did you ever have a day where you felt that you were moving from one mistaken decision to another all day long?

> In the movie *Groundhog Day*, Bill Murray plays Phil, a grouchy weatherman, who is trapped in the perpetual bad day. Phil is sent to Punxsutawney, PA, on February 2 to cover the annual groundhog festival, a superstitious ritual that is supposed to predict the length of the remaining winter. Phil wakes up early to find that his shower has no hot water and the day is downhill from there, until to top it off, he is forced by a snowstorm to spend a second night in Punxsutawney. The next morning, when he wakes, he finds no relief as events of the previous day begin to repeat themselves. Phil becomes trapped in a time loop, and he seems condemned to relive the same miserable day over and over again.
>
> The movie traces the progression of Phil's response not only to the situation of being stuck in the repeating nightmare, but more importantly to the different stimuli happening around him. The plot of the movie is that Phil is condemned to keep repeating this one day until he gets it 100% right.

As each day repeats itself, Phil is presented with the same circumstances. Through a process of trial and error, he gets to see which responses bring him the most satisfying results. It is the cumulative effect of how Phil responds to all the details of his day, from the little annoyances, such as a lack of hot water, to the deeper issues of how he relates to other human beings, which determine the effectiveness of his living that day. The nightmare ends and Phil is released to move on, when he learns how to make all the right choices.

In our lives, unfortunately, we do not have the opportunity to keep repeating our actions until we get them all right. We have to live with the consequences of each bad decision. In the movie, as in life, our bad days are a product of our mistaken responses to the stimuli that we come across. A good day is one where we chose the most satisfying and pleasurable responses to the circumstances we encounter.

We are all driven by the desire for pleasure, but we make mistakes about how to achieve it. This is because we have not learned what pleasures are available in life. So we end up confused, not knowing what we really want or how to get it. Therefore, we take a lot of wrong turns. The "C" of life is that we are mistake prone and coming to a realization of this quandary is the first step to learning to choose more effectively.

Exercises ~

❶ Some theologians and philosophers would quarrel with the claim that people are mistake-prone. An alternative theory might be that by nature people are sinners. In your opinion which theory—sin or mistake—is more accurate and why? Do you have an alternative theory?

❷ Reflect on your own views on the concept of sin.

❸ Think of a specific misdeed that you have done or wrong action you have taken. Analyze your motivation and the results of the action. Which best describes the event: sin or mistake? Why?

❹ View the movie *Groundhog Day*. According to the movie's plot, what factors go into making Phil's perfect day? Do you agree with these factors, or would you have written in other factors for the perfect day?

❺ Imagine that you are a lawyer, and you represent a female client in drafting a will. In the course of representation, you learn that the client is HIV positive, but she has not informed her partner. The professional code allows for lawyers to reveal client confidences in cases of imminent bodily harm, but the odds of a male getting HIV from a female are very low. What do you do? How would you characterize the female clients actions in this case—is she making a mistake, committing a sin, doing the right thing? How would you justify her behavior?

The "D" of Life: Decision-Making Requires Education

What is the worst mistake that you can make? Murder? Murder is a terrible mistake. What about thievery, incest, or treason? Is there something even worse?

> If the root of all evil, so to speak, is making mistakes, then it logically follows that the worst mistake—the most dangerous, destructive, painful, and contagious disease of all—is ignorance. After all, ignorance is the foundation of all mistakes.

If we really had the opportunity to live each day over and over again until we learned to get it right, then our progression through life would be based on a certain knowledge of which decision is best at any given moment. Since we do not have the benefit of such a training process, we are left to tackle each real life situation based on our limited current knowledge.

Moreover, since our decisions in life are driven by a motivation for pleasure, when you do not know what pleasure is, you are likely to end up searching in the wrong places and end up so confused that you run the risk of ruining not only your own life, but that of somebody else as well.

Obviously then, making decisions in a vacuum, with limited knowledge and out of ignorance, is the worst mistake you could possibly make, since it will lead to disaster both for you and for those around you. This is the worst kind of ignorance.

The antidote to ignorance is education! This is the "D" of life—get an education.

But will a formal education, the kind that most people receive in university, provide the solution? Well, that's not what I'm talking about here.

The education I'm talking about is not generally taught in a school. Universities purport to teach their students how to think, but as students engross themselves in subjects like calculus, literature, biology, history, and geography, they often neglect to relate this information to their behavior as human beings. As students learn about functions and independent variables, the process of osmosis, the trajectory of planetary orbits, and about the shape of Australia and when and why its land mass was torn off the Indian continent, they can easily miss the point that this information is meant to make them better people.

This observation is not meant to devalue the acquisition of knowledge for its own sake, since knowledge of the world is central to our ability to make informed decisions. Without factual and conceptual knowledge, we cannot progress as a society. Nevertheless, when the process is complete, are students, even those within the humanities, any closer to knowing who they are? After 12 years of primary education, four years as undergraduates, and who knows how many as graduate students, have the products of formal education come to any conclusions about why they were created or for what purpose they are living?

Well, it varies from person to person, but individuals who do not know the answers to those questions, really do not know themselves; and if they do not know themselves, they really do not know much of anything.

There are countless examples throughout history of civilizations that were cultured and educated, but made the most terrible mistakes because of greed, apathy and cruelty. Western civilization has its roots in Greece and Rome. Our legal system, our literature, and our art, and our architecture are all traced back to this civilization, and we take pride in this fact.

Nevertheless, what did members of this civilization do for sport on Sunday afternoon? They went to the Coliseum to watch condemned men, women and children tear each other apart. Germany prior to WWII represented the height of European culture, and a majority of the death camp commanders had PhDs or were medical doctors.

> Ignorance is not just a matter of not knowing facts. The worst ignorance, the kind that leads people to the most painful mistakes, is ignorance about life.

Exercises~

❶ Do you think there is a correlation between a person's level of formal education and whether he or she acts ethically? Is there a connection between how cultured a person is and how moral a person is? Can morality be taught at all? Should it be a goal of a formal education? How could something like that be implemented?

❷ List two classes that you have taken in your college (or high school) career that have had a significant impact in the way you view reality. Have these courses also impacted on the way that you live your life, or how you approach decision-making? Do you feel that these classes have helped you to become a more ethical and moral person? If so, describe why and how.

❸ What would you say is the purpose of life? How does your life fit into this purpose?

❹ List the five most pleasurable experiences that you have ever had. Can you imagine a more pleasurable experience? If so, what would it be? What would you do if someone you trusted told you that they had had an experience so profound and so pleasurable that it far exceeded anything they had previously encountered or thought was possible (and it is legal!)?

So what kind of education are we talking about? An education about LIFE. An education about how to make good and effective *informed* decisions. To avoid mistakes and achieve our potential, we need an education about our own lives.

Understanding Begins With the ABCs

There is a lot to learn about life! In this chapter we have covered the ABCs:

* Ultimately, all people are motivated by a single factor—pleasure.

* People acquire knowledge and beliefs to the extent that they accept information conveyed to them as true, and this information ends up determining who they are and how they behave. Therefore, all people are responsible for critically analyzing information they obtain.

* You cannot begin your quest for the highest level of pleasure until you agree that it is possible for you to transcend your present circumstances in order to do this. The

first step is for you to investigate and judge the validity of the assumptions underlying your actions.

* The root of all problems is making mistakes, mistakenly choosing a course of action on the belief that it will lead to the greatest level of pleasure, when in reality a different course of action would have been more satisfying.

* The greatest mistake of all is not taking the time to get an education, to find out what life is all about, to find out what will provide you with the greatest level of pleasure.

The ultimate mistake is not taking the responsibility to investigate what life is all about, to discover its greatest pleasure, and how is it obtained. If everything we do is motivated by the desire for pleasure, then the purpose of life must be to find the path that leads to the deepest, most long-lasting, and most meaningful pleasures. Exploring this path will be the subject of the next chapter.

chapter 2

the Five Levels *of* Pleasure

Most people simply do not know what life has to offer. And if you do not know what is available, if you don't know how to get the most out of living, then how are you supposed to find true happiness?

I'm not going to kid you: Finding true happiness requires work. No pain, no gain. But it is absolutely within the grasp of every person, including you. You simply need to understand what it is, as well as understand the path to attaining it. Once you know all of the pleasures available to a person, you can get there.

This chapter will introduce you to the five different levels of pleasure available to a human being, and will show you what you need to do in order to become a connoisseur of each of them. In fact, this chapter will show you how to become a connoisseur of each level of pleasure, from "Fifth Class" to "First Class," and how to put this recognition to work in the pursuit of successful decision-making and ultimate happiness.

Measuring Pleasure

How is pleasure measured and categorized, anyway?

As I pointed out in the previous chapter, parents want their children to be happy. However, we all recognize that parents want more than simple happiness for their children. Parents want their children to enjoy a range of pleasures. Parents certainly want their children to enjoy good food, vacations, sports, nice cloths, and music, and in addition, parents want their children to enjoy deeper pleasures.

Aiming for more than just a good steak and a game of tennis, parents want their children to have good careers, and they generally want them to get married and to have children of their own. Parents know the deep sense of joy and satisfaction that comes with these experiences. Certainly, they recognize that playing tennis is fun, but if at age 30 your child does not want to work or get married, but only to play tennis all day and go to the club at night, then as a parent you might feel pretty frustrated. Parents want children to develop themselves and to achieve their potential. These pleasures exist on a different plane.

Imagine that a parent was aware of all the pleasures available to a human being. Then, one day, by chance, this person discovered a new experience that was far more enriching and fulfilling than any previously known. Unquestionably, he or she would do all in their power to relive the experience. Moreover, he or she would try to share this knowledge with their children, and teach them how to attain the same pleasure. He or she would still want the kids to continue to enjoy playing tennis and going to the club, but now the focus would be on a different class, *a different level*, of pleasure.

Classes of Pleasure

Airlines generally have three classes of service, but what if they had five? And what if these classes of service could be compared to classes of pleasure? Consider the possibilities:

The best way to travel is first class. Given the choice and the money, everyone would all prefer to fly first class.

What is second best? Second class!? Of course no airline calls it "second class." Instead, they use euphemisms like *business class, executive class*, and even *ambassador class*. Nobody wants to think of themselves as traveling second class, especially when paying an extra several hundred dollars for the privilege, even though that is in actuality what it really is!

Third class is called *tourist, coach,* or *economy class*—but never "third class." Here people are usually packed in like sardines and pay for whatever food might be available.

What about fourth class? If such a thing existed on airplanes, it might be located down below with the animals in the baggage compartment.

And fifth class? Maybe the airlines would provide a rope and say, "Hang on!" The traveler would still get from here to there, but certainly there would have to be a better way.

So too in life, people can fly in various classes, and it goes without saying that everybody wants to travel first class. Unfortunately, most people never find out how. They travel their whole lives in fifth class, just barely hanging on, and the sad thing is sometimes life becomes too hard for them and they just let go.

Not too long ago, a book entitled *Final Exit*[1] sold around a million copies in the United States and was on *The New York Times* Best Seller list for a number of months. *Final Exit* is a book about how to commit suicide in the comfort of your own home. People do not buy this book because it makes for fascinating reading; it is a technical manual. People want it on their shelves just in case they want to let go. The popularity of this book shows us that there are a great many people in the world who are just not getting the kinds of pleasures that make the effort of life worth living.

No Exchange Rate

Unlike the classes of service on an airline, however, from one class of pleasure to another, you cannot purchase an upgrade. This is the distinguishing characteristic separating one class of pleasure from another; from one class of pleasure to another there is no exchange rate.

By way of analogy, there are many types of currencies in the world—dollars, pounds, euros, yen—but they all essentially represent the same thing. They all can be exchanged one for the other, albeit at

---

[1] Humphry, Derek. *Final Exit: The Practicalities of Self-Deliverance and Assisted Suicide for the Dying.* Dell Paperbacks (New York, 1997).

varying rates. When it comes to different classes of pleasure, on the other hand, a million units of fifth class pleasure cannot acquire for you a single unit of fourth-class pleasure, and no amount of fourth-class pleasure can acquire a unit of third class pleasure, and so on. Each class is non-exchangeable. There is no exchange rate.

Transcending the Levels of Pleasure

I'm going to show you how each successive level of the Five Levels of Pleasure is so qualitatively superior to the previous level that it is non-exchangeable. However, before we can delve into a description of these levels, and indeed before you can access the pleasure available at any level, you have to sensitize yourself to three aspects of pleasure: 1) to truly enjoy any pleasure requires becoming a connoisseur; 2) pleasure requires focus; and 3) pleasure requires discernment.

Become a Connoisseur

In a wine-tasting course, you quickly learn that a glass of wine is far more than a liquid that wets your mouth. There are a whole variety of pleasures available in every glass of wine. There is the bouquet, the color, the texture, and, believe it or not, there are actually many parts of the mouth with which to taste the wine, each part providing a totally different taste experience. However, many people are totally unaware of the richness available in a glass of wine.

Similarly, life offers a lot of different opportunities for pleasure. A beautiful day could give you hours of pleasure if you sensitize yourself to all of its exquisite details. Without learning to do that, its beauty gives you a lift only for a matter of minutes and then the feeling is gone.

> Within each level of pleasure, you have to learn how to appreciate and enjoy the pleasure available to you; otherwise, you cannot access the pleasure.

Just as someone cannot fully appreciate the pleasures of a glass of wine without a wine tasting course, or the painting of a great master without an art appreciation class, you cannot fully enjoy the entire spectrum of life's pleasures without knowing what those pleasures are and learning to savor them.

Focus on the Pleasure, Not the Effort

Every pleasure in life has a price tag attached to it. This price tag is effort. Moreover, the greater the pleasure, the greater the price, the greater the effort needed to acquire it.

Superficial pleasures require far less effort to attain. The effort involved in winning a game of tic-tac-toe is nothing like the effort involved in winning a marathon, and there is no comparison between the pleasure that each of the victors receives.

In addition, to truly appreciate any pleasure, you have to learn to focus on that pleasure and not on the price tag associated with it. If you focus on the pleasure, you will not notice the effort; but if you focus on the effort, you will not notice the pleasure.

Take a group of teenagers who love to play basketball. On a good Sunday afternoon, they might play ball for two or three hours without interruption. But, what might happen if we ask them to conduct the following experiment:

> Play basketball as you would normally, but we are going to take away the ball. We want you to run, jump, shoot, defend against each other, as you would if you were really playing.

For how long would they play? Five minutes, ten minutes? Very shortly, they would start wondering, "What's the point? Why are we being put through this exercise?" They would begin complaining, "Hey, what are you doing to us? We've had enough of this!"

Give them back the ball, and they might continue playing for hours.

Similarly, in life, you have to keep your eye on the ball. You have to learn to focus on the pleasure. When you do, you do not notice the effort. If you do not focus on the pleasure, however, you are playing basketball without the ball. Every movement takes enormous effort.

At each level of pleasure, you have a choice: Focus on the pleasure; or focus on the effort. Focus on the effort, and you will not even want to get out of bed. Focus on the pleasure, and no amount of effort will deter you.

Beware of Counterfeit Pleasures

The third prerequisite in recognizing and moving up through the five levels of pleasure is to *beware of counterfeit pleasures*. Imagine someone left $100,000 on your doorstep. You would be ecstatic! You might walk into Tiffany's to buy yourself a few watches, and you would still have a good $90,000 left. You would feel great. That is until you bump into the two policemen waiting for you at the door. What happened? *Nothing in life comes for free; you got counterfeit money.*

Just as there is counterfeit money, there are counterfeit pleasures. People make mistakes all the time thinking they are going to have pleasure but wind up with something less.

> **Within each level of pleasure, there is a counterfeit experience that says, "Come vest your time and energy trying to attain me." In the end, however, you are duped by an illusion masquerading as true pleasure.**

The pursuit of pleasure should be treated as serious business. A person has to be businesslike in the effort to achieve it. If someone came into a businessperson's office and said, "I have a great idea to help you make ten million dollars. Just invest a few hundred thousand dollars in me to get it going," a businessperson would not say, "Great. Let's go." A businessperson would investigate.

Similarly, if we really want pleasure, then we have to make sure that when we invest our most precious resources, our time and energy, we are pursuing real pleasure and not a counterfeit.

The Biggest Counterfeit Pleasure

There is one counterfeit pleasure that inhibits our attaining real pleasure more than any other.

Consider this: What is the opposite of pain?

When asked this question the overwhelming majority of people answer, "Pleasure." This, however, is not true! The opposite of pain is *no pain*, or *comfort*. And comfort is NOT pleasure. It is only *no pain*.

To many of us, the ultimate pleasure is a vacation in Hawaii—lying on the warm sand, a cool breeze wafting through the air, a tall drink right next to us, every muscle in our bodies completely relaxed. We are so relaxed that we are almost falling, falling, falling asleep—but we cannot let ourselves! If we do, we miss the whole experience. Boy, that is living! Or is it? Is to be almost asleep really living?

Comfort is nice—it is a painless experience—but it is not pleasure.

> **In truth, pain is the price we pay for pleasure. Anything in life that is really worthwhile—good relationships, successful careers, the pursuit of meaning—all of life's lasting pleasures require pain and effort to achieve.**

If a person wants to graduate from college in order to get a good job, he or she has to work hard and sometimes to study late into the night to pass final exams. The pain of some sleepless nights is the price of a diploma. If someone wants to keep fit to have the pleasure of running a marathon, he or she has to train and experience the pain of sore muscles to attain that pleasure. If a person wants to be a gold-medal Olympic champion, he or she is not going to get there on a beach in Hawaii.

To understand the relationship between pain and pleasure, let's return to our example of parents: If we ask parents what their greatest pleasure is, they most probably will answer that it is their children. If we then ask, what their greatest pain is, again they will most likely answer that it is their children. It is not an accident that a person's greatest pleasure is also the thing that takes the greatest amount of pain and effort to attain.

If we pursue comfort, it is true that we will be rid of pain, but we will also be robbed of almost any type of achievement. If we try to get at pleasure by spending our lives avoiding pain, we will only end up with this counterfeit: comfort. Without effort, we will never get real pleasure. One of the most telltale signs of a counterfeit pleasure is this anomaly—it comes for free. The real thing definitely has a price tag.

Indeed, not all pleasures are created equal. Some are qualitatively superior to others. To experience the full pleasure available at each level: (1) you have to become a connoisseur of that pleasure; (2) you have to focus on the pleasure; and (3) you have to beware of its counterfeit.

Exercises~

❶ Consider the most pleasurable events in your life over the past few years. List the top five (or ten)! Rank them! What effort, if any, was involved in their achievement?

❷ You go to a dinner party, and your host serves you an exotic delicacy that you have never seen before, but it strikes you as repulsive (e.g. sweetbreads, aka cow brains, or fresh turtle meat), do you try it? If you do not try it, do you think that you will be missing out on one of life's pleasures? What if your host assures you that it is their favorite dish, it has the most extraordinary taste you will ever encounter, and it is the traditional food of their home country set aside to honor special guests?

Fifth Class Pleasure: Let's Get Physical

Fifth class pleasure is the most basic and available. Countless experiences fall into the category of physical pleasure. If you can smell it, touch it, taste it, see it, or hear it—and it gives you pleasure—then chances are that it is a fifth class pleasure.

Humans exist in a physical world. The physical world is our habitat, so it is only natural that we enjoy it. Have you ever stopped to be amazed at the array of pleasures that are available in something as simple and natural as a piece of fruit? Take an apple for example. Did you ever notice how attractive it is—a beautiful Red Delicious apple. Then there is its texture, smooth to touch. Smell it; it is sweet. Bite into it, and it is tasty and crunchy. And with all this, it is healthy too. It gives you vitamins and energy.

The whole world is filled with such pleasures. The scenery in which we live is breathtaking—rivers and waterfalls, mountains and vistas, stars and an expansive sky—and it all serves us so perfectly well. Even something as intensely physical as intimate relations is at the same time pleasurable and profoundly beneficial. People have biological, emotional and physical drives to connect with one another, and we have been designed to enjoy this process immensely. So we should eat and enjoy!

However, is there a difference between tasting the good fruits of the world and gorging on them? Is there such a thing *as too much of a good thing?*

The Counterfeit—Self-Indulgence and Comfort

The counterfeits of fifth class pleasure are self-indulgence and comfort. Wine is wonderful in moderation, but guzzling down an entire bottle could make you throw up. Salty foods taste great, but if you make a steady diet of them, you are likely to end up with high blood pressure.

If you partake of fifth class pleasure without awareness, without savoring it, for the mere purpose of tantalizing your senses as an end in itself, you will end up feeling bloated, overstuffed, and drained of energy. After that sense of immediate gratification, you feel lowered by the experience. This is not an argument for asceticism or celibacy, for these same pleasures have the potential to leave a person invigorated.

The key to avoiding the trap of self-indulgence, though, is awareness. When you are aware, you do not allow your appetite to rule over you. Then, you are able to maximize your fifth class pleasure experience.

Exercises~

❶ Some religions encourage asceticism and look negatively upon partaking of physical pleasures. In ancient Greece, the prevailing culture was hedonistic—one obsessed with aesthetics and material pleasure. The naked human body was celebrated and the gods themselves represented physical excess. Sensory pleasure was an ideal. Is there any merit to either approach to life? Is this *the* ideal?

❷ You have won a one-night stay at a famous resort spa, and your prize includes a gift certificate for a $150. Your gift certificate will buy a gourmet dinner at the spa's internationally acclaimed restaurant or a massage and body treatment at the spa's health center. Which do you choose? Is there a different pleasure that you would like to spend your certificate on? What factors go into making the decision? Are these options interchangeable—meaning could you just as easily chose one over the other, or if someone paid you $50 would you chose the other option instead? Suppose you chose the massage, would you change your mind if an old friend were to be seated at your table? If so, why?

❸ On a piece of paper make five columns, one for each of your five senses. In each column make a list of some of the pleasures that these senses provide you with. Consider how fortunate you are, because not everyone in life has mastery over all five of their senses.

❹ Imagine that you had to give up either your power of sight or your hearing. Which would it be? Imagine that you had to choose between your sense of touch and taste. Which would you chose? Finally, consider whether you would trade your sense of smell for $25 million dollars. Ask a few friends about these choices to see what they say.

❺ Standard medical practice today includes "genetic" counseling when pregnant women meet for an initial consultation with their obstetrician. Genetic counseling includes in utero testing for various genetic deceases, such as Down syndrome, and therapeutic abortions, if the parents decide that bringing a child with such a disease into the world is not desired based on "quality of life" considerations for the prospective child. If you were the hospital ethicist, and prenatal testing showed genetic defect indicating that a fetus would be born deaf and blind, would you recommend a therapeutic abortion?

Fourth Class Pleasure: Money Can't Buy It

As we have said, there are five classes of pleasure in the plane flight of life. So far we have described only fifth class, and so long as we have not become involved with its counterfeit, we have advocated physical and material pleasures as good and positive. However, fifth class is still only fifth class—at this level we are holding onto the rope outside the plane. Now, it is time to climb aboard and to begin experiencing some of the more serious pleasures that life has to offer.

Remember, we are now going to describe a new class of pleasure, and the distinguishing facet of a new class is *no exchange rate*. No amount of fifth class pleasure—physical and material pleasure—will be able to acquire even a single unit of fourth class pleasure.

What do you imagine that it is? What could it be? To discover fourth class pleasure, ask yourself: What is worth more than all the physical and material pleasure in the world combined; what is something that most people are willing to sacrifice materially in order to attain; what is something that money just cannot buy?

As sung by the Beatles: "Money can't buy me love." Fourth class pleasure is love.

In case you doubt this, let us examine how we can know that it is true—that love is qualitatively more pleasurable than all physical pleasures combined, that love is worth more than all the money in the world.

> Imagine that a very wealthy individual approaches the parents of a small child (perhaps your parents when you were little), and this person offers, "Look here, I have all the money in the world, but I am childless. I'll give you $50 million for your child. No strings attached. Nothing will happen to them. They will have the best of everything. There is only one condition: We will move to another country, and you will never see or hear from your child again. You won't get a postcard. You won't know anything about him or her. But, you'll get fifty million dollars free and clear." Would the parents take it? Would your parents take it?

Of course not! Not for $50 million—a mind-boggling amount of fifth class pleasure. No amount of money could induce a parent to sell a child. (Parents who give their children up for adoption do so out of love, not for the monetary reward. They believe that by doing such an act, they are doing the best thing possible.) There is no exchange rate from fifth class to fourth class pleasure. The pleasure of love, of relationships, cannot be traded for any amount of material gain.

Consider the scene now, what would be the reaction of a parent, having just turned down $50 million, when this parent sees her child walk into the room? She would likely stare in amazement. Perhaps, she would run to hug and kiss the child. Without a doubt, she would think to herself with newfound awareness, "What is this creature that's worth more than all that money?"

Now let us say that the parent in our story is a lawyer, working 60 to 70 hours a week trying to reach her professional goals, killing herself to make money, and all this time she has a fortune at home worth more than all the money she will ever earn. How much time do you suppose this lawyer spends each week with her child? Maybe, she spends a couple of hours a week in total with her fortune.

Having just turned down the $50 million and coming to a new realization that she already possesses a treasure, this parent might think that she should change her priorities. She might call her boss and say that she is taking the two weeks vacation that the firm owes her in order to spend a much-earned break with her family.

Once this is settled, the parent needs to figure out what to do with her treasure during this time off. She might take her child to the park, read a few stories, and go to the ice cream shop. For the first few hours this works fine; the parent and child have a great time. A little while later, though, the day begins to grow tedious, especially when the child begins to get cranky and over-tired and our lawyer begins to get aggravated.

When the lawyer finally manages to get her little one home, she then has to face all of the typical struggles of parenting. Even working together with her spouse, dinnertime is a disaster; the child will not eat or throws food on the floor. Bath time almost results in destroying the hallway carpet. Bedtime is like War of the Worlds. (Have you ever noticed that a great many children's book end with the main character going to sleep? Everyone is hoping that the power of suggestion will work!)

Finally, at 10 p.m., when our lawyer collapses on the couch, she turns to her spouse and says, "Maybe it was a little irresponsible of me to have acted so impetuously in taking two weeks off. I'm so busy at work. The right thing to do is to go back to work tomorrow morning."

We Need a Course in Love Tasting

What is this lawyer's problem? Simple: She is not a connoisseur. She has not truly learned what love is and how to enjoy its pleasure. You can only tickle your children for so long, after all. This lawyer does not need a course in wine tasting; she needs a course in love tasting!

Our lawyer knows that her child is more valuable than $50 million. The child represents a class of pleasure no money can buy. Yet, she does not know how to enjoy this pleasure.

To appreciate love, you must first understand it. Without a clear understanding of the nature of love, our lawyer focuses only on the pain and effort involved in raising her child. In a sense, she is playing basketball without the ball.

> Love is the emotional pleasure that results from focusing on the virtues of another person.

If our lawyer can understand this and learns to focus her attention in this way, then even while the food is flying across the kitchen table, she can still love and discipline her child, both at the same time. *The key to success is not eliminating the pain; that is impossible. Rather, it is to focus on the pleasure that results from all the effort.*

The Price of Love is Commitment

If you want to love someone, there is a price you have to pay. That price is commitment. To begin to love someone, you have to make the effort to understand that person's virtues. You have to make a decision that you are going to focus on this person's virtues and not their shortcomings.

> Every human being is a mixed bag of strengths and weaknesses. If you focus on their virtues, you will come to love them; if you focus on their shortcomings, you will not want to spend five minutes with them.

The real effort of loving a person is not to find their virtues—
everyone has virtues. The real effort is making the commitment and
taking the responsibility to focus on their virtues and not their
shortcomings.

To see the truth of this aspect of love, consider how an expectant
mother or father would respond to the query of whether they
intend to love their children. They would respond, "of course we
do." And if we would then point out to these expectant parents that
they have no idea of what kind of people their children will turn out
to be, that perhaps their offspring will end up as brats like the neigh-
bor's kid down the street, the parents will respond that they will love
their children nonetheless. They would not say, "Well, we'll have
kids, get to know them, and decide afterward based on their person-
alities if we want to keep them or not." That would obviously be
ridiculous. Parents are naturally committed to loving any children
they have, so they do. This is true, in spite of any weaknesses that
they notice. This is true no matter what their children do.

> In December 2000, a man walked into a computer-consulting
> firm in a suburb of Boston with an arsenal of guns and explo-
> sives, and proceeded to massacre seven people. Afterward in an
> interview, the man's parents expressed tremendous remorse and
> dismay over the incident, yet clearly, they still deeply cared for
> their son. The same pattern is evident in the interviews with the
> parents of children involved in school shootings, as well as the
> parents of murderers on death row. Parents are absolutely com-
> mitted to loving their children.

Which relationship might one suspect to work more success-
fully—the relationship between spouses or the relationship between
parents and children? Logically, one might expect to see fewer
breakups between husbands and wives than between parents and
children. Our spouse is someone *we choose* to marry, while our chil-
dren are accidents of birth. Still, nobody divorces their children, but
people frequently divorce their spouses. This is, because the commit-
ment to love is natural between parent and child, whereas it has to
be earned between husband and wife. If a person does not make the
effort of commitment, everything a person's spouse does will get on

their nerves and drive them up a wall—whereas the same things when done by that same person's children are accepted and would never lead them to consider getting rid of them.

Love's Counterfeit: Infatuation

The third prerequisite to enjoying any pleasure is being watchful of the counterfeit. The great counterfeit of love is the notion that it is effort-free. The concept that love is not something one chooses, but rather something that a person falls into. In reality, though, this notion that love just happens is a lie. This is the counterfeit of love; this is infatuation.

This romantic vision of love is a legacy bequeathed to us by Greek mythology and represented by the character Cupid. It is the notion conveyed in books and movies that love does not require pain, effort, and a lot of hard work; but rather that love is a magical and mystical happening.

> Two people are alone in a park, walking beneath the full moon. Soft music is playing in the background. Cupid sneaks up behind them and shoots them with an arrow. Now they are hopelessly in love. They get married, and ride off into the sunset. Then, real life begins. Eventually they have kids, a big house, and a bigger mortgage. Eventually, to pay the bills, the husband has to work late at night. One night, at work, the husband is sending an email to his administrative assistant, and Cupid sneaks up and shoots him again. Now, he is in love with his employee. He comes back to his wife and says, "What can I do, honey? That bum shot me again! I fell in love with the admin." Out goes the wife and in comes the assistant, and they are off again riding into the sunset.

This is a modern vision of romantic love. We are victims of love— easy come, easy go. That initial spark is everything; it is the only important aspect of the story. In this vision, how does one keep a marriage together? One hopes that Cupid does not shoot them again!

There is one sure test to know if you are truly in love or infatuated. When you catch yourself saying, "He's perfect" or "She's perfect," then beware! This certainly is not reality, and it is a sure sign of infatuation.

In life, there is no such thing as effort-free loving. This is a counterfeit; this is infatuation and lust. Only committed love is really forever. Real love takes work, but if you want that pleasure, it is available in every relationship. You just have to be willing to pay the price.

Exercises~

❶ While philosophers have grappled with the topics of ethics and morality, poets have always sung of love. Poets have also written about death, childhood, nature, and war, but more than anything else, about love. Why do you think this is so? Find several poems about love, or the lyrics to some popular songs, for reading and discussion in small groups. What aspect of love do these speak about—pleasure, pain, happiness, physical attraction? Are any of the poems, or song lyrics, really speaking about infatuation? Do any of these speak about how to keep love alive? Do any provide you with a definition of love?

❷ Consider whether you ever thought you were "in love." Was this real love or infatuation? How do you know?

❸ Consider whether you want to be in love now. What do you want to get out of the loving relationship? What are you prepared to give to it?

❹ Think of one loving relationship that you would like to improve. Make a list of all the positive traits of your partner in that relationship. Review this list every couple of days for two weeks. At the end of two weeks, do you feel that your bond with this person has increased?

Third Class Pleasure: The "More" to Life

So far we have identified two levels of pleasure: physical or material pleasure and love. Now as great a pleasure as love is, we realize that it is not the ultimate purpose of life. If someone were to tell you that they wanted to marry you in order to spend the entire day focusing on your virtues, you would wonder, "Is this guy obsessed. Doesn't he have anything else to do with his life? There's more to life than just me (even if I am something special)."

So what is that "more" in life?

Remember, from one class of pleasure to another, there is no exchange rate. No amount of fourth class pleasure, no amount of love, can buy an ounce of third class pleasure. So think for a moment, what is greater then love?

To answer the question definitively, consider whether there is anything in the world that would compel a person to give up what they love. Think about it, what compels parents to give up their children; what do parents sacrifice their children for?

A cause. A cause, the drive for meaning, is greater than love. Look around the world, look to the Middle East, look to Iraq and Afghanistan, look to our own country's not too distant past. Parents are willing to sacrifice their children for a cause, for the needs of the nation.

> Third class pleasure is conviction. People will die themselves for a reason, for an idea, that they consider has more value than their own lives. This is evidence that all the love in the world and all the money in the world are not worth one moment of third class pleasure. It is weightier; it is in a different class.

Third class pleasure is conviction. If we take a closer look, we will see that it is also the drive to do good and be good—to have self-worth. It is the desire to make a difference in the world. These things are very heavy. To illustrate the truth of this point, contemplate the following hypothetical: Imagine you are on a plane or cruise ship, which is hijacked by terrorists. They come to you and hand you a knife. They say, "either you kill these 500 innocent people or we'll kill you." What would you do? Could you kill 500 innocent men, women, and children?

You could not do it. Even though you have a loving wife and five kids you adore, you still could not kill 500 innocent people. Even if the terrorists say that they will kill not you but your wife and children, you still would not be able to take 500 innocent lives—you would not even be able to take one innocent life!

Wow! Think about that for a moment!

Why not? Why are you not able to take these innocent lives?

Because it is wrong!

Wait a minute! You have done other wrong things in your life, so what is the big deal now? Do just one more wrong thing.

The reason that you would not be able to do such a horrendous act is because it is too wrong. Such an act would strike at the essence of your being. To do such an act, you would sacrifice any semblance that you have of yourself as a human being; you would be sacrificing the pleasure of being good. After such an act, you would not be able to live with yourself. You would go mad. Every human needs and wants to be good, and it would be impossible to consider yourself as good after committing an utterly evil act! Therefore, death becomes an alternative.

Consider the implications of what this means! People are willing to give up all that they possess in physical and material pleasures and in love for the pleasure of being good. This indicates that conviction is heavier. It is more. Being good and doing the right thing are profound pleasures. They are in a higher class.

Discovering Conviction

The issue now is how do we acquire this pleasure. To enjoy the pleasure of being good, to revel in that pleasure, we need a class in "good tasting." Generally, people do not know how to enjoy *being* good. Generally, we only enjoy being good *in retrospect*.

A number of years ago in Columbus, Ohio, the door of an armored car opened and out came two million dollars.[2] Well, as you can imagine, dozens of people made a grab for the money. The company only recovered about $100,000 of the cash. A few days later a man returned $57,000. An amazing thing! So amazing that it made the newspapers and reporters interviewed this man's friends and relatives to see what kind of person would do such a good deed. People they interviewed called him a fool. His own father said, "I thought I raised [him] better than that." A co-worker commented, "that was a gift from God and [he] gave it back."

Imagine, not stealing is considered foolish! Now think about this man. How difficult a decision was it for him to return the money? This act may have been the most difficult decision of his life, and he probably got little satisfaction at the time. In retrospect, however, he can live with the profound satisfaction that he did the right thing.

The reason that doing good is often pleasurable only in retrospect is because the effort, the cost involved in being good, is so intense at the moment of the act that it usually obscures our ability to appreciate the pleasure of being good at the time. In retrospect, however, at the end of the day, once the pain of carrying out your responsibilities has past, you can now objectively look back and appreciate the pleasure and the conviction of being good, of what you accomplished.

The cost, the price of goodness, is courage. Courage is that quality of mind which enables a person to encounter difficulties and maintain their values.

Think about the last time that someone at a checkout register gave you an extra dollar in change. Remember the pain you experienced at that moment, when deciding whether to inform the clerk? Then remember the tremendous feeling of satisfaction you had afterward, when the clerk smiled at you and extolled your virtues as if you were the only honest person to have ever walked this earth? It felt great did it not? But that feeling only came in retrospect.

One way to develop the skill of appreciating third class pleasure is to sit down at the end of every day, when the effort of what you

---

[2] Bowen, Ezra. "What Ever Became of Honest Abe?" *Time*, vol. 131, Apr. 4, 1988, p. 68.

have done is behind you, and focus your attention on what you did that was good and meaningful. The more you practice that, the more you will become a connoisseur of being good, and eventually you will be able to get that same pleasure even while you are under the pressure of the moment.

Another way to develop the skill of appreciating third class pleasure is to seriously consider what you are willing to live for. From our discussion thus far, it is clear that there are some things for which we are willing to die. We are all willing to die to be good. Indeed, for each of us there is some cause, for which we would be willing to sacrifices our lives. So, the question arises, do we have the courage to live for the same cause?

Many people would believe that they would fight to protect their country, but in their everyday lives they focus on their own insular world without any connection to this cause in the least. Maybe they give a few dollars to a charity related to the cause, or maybe on Election Day, they will show up to vote. Nonetheless, through the daily grind of living, they are not really in touch with these issues, even though they're important.

> There is a famous story about Alfred Nobel, the creator of the Nobel Prize. When Mr. Nobel's brother died, the newspapers got the story wrong, and printed Alfred Nobel's obituary by mistake. Until that time, Mr. Nobel was best known as the inventor of dynamite, and his obituary described him as a person who brought great misery and destruction to the world. Shocked by this picture of himself, Nobel committed himself to finding a greater cause to live for. With this in mind, he created the Nobel Prize to celebrate positive human achievement.

How do you want successive generations to view your life? How do you want your children to remember you?

> **To become a connoisseur of third class pleasure, you first need to know what you would be willing to die for.**

More importantly, once you have identified this source of conviction and pleasure, you need to commit yourself to living for it as well. Until then, you have not really begun living.

As a connoisseur of third class pleasure, you need to know what you are willing to live for. Until you find that cause, all you are chasing is fifth class and fourth class pleasure. You are not living life to the hilt; you have not really made it. Third class pleasure is above the other two—it is self-respect, it is value, it is conviction.

The Counterfeit—Just "Looking Good"

In your search for meaning, you have to be careful. There is always the counterfeit. In this class of pleasure, the counterfeit of being good is "looking good." If you do not know what genuine good is, then you are likely to expend a lot of effort trying to win the admiration of society in order to make yourself feel important.

The most prevalent counterfeit coin for "good" in the United States is financial success. If you're not financially successful, even if you're a good spouse, a good friend, and a loyal human being, you can still be considered a failure. In our culture there is an incessant need to keep up with the Joneses, and if we cannot buy our spouses that nice new car or designer outfit, we are each somehow less of a human being. Even though on some level everybody knows that people can succeed financially and still be the dregs of society, most of us somewhere at the root of our psyche still believe that if we have not succeeded financially, we have not made it in life.

Beware not to fall into this trap. If you do, then despite how good you are as a spouse or a friend or a person, you will never achieve a true feeling of self-worth. Do not fall for just "looking good." Deeds are the genuine articles, and they should provide us with the self-respect that we all crave. It is a basic energy that we all require. If we do not have self-respect, we die.

Everyone needs meaning in life. You can have a lot of fifth class pleasure—vacations, a dream home, designer clothing—and you can even have plenty of fourth class pleasure—a wonderful spouse and children—and yet still have moments in your life when you may say "What's it all for! I didn't do anything."

Do you ever wonder why so many of the rich and famous, people with huge houses and gardens, yachts and skiing holidays, and whose children go to the best schools, drift from marriage to marriage, or from drug to drug, or even commit suicide? These people seemingly have everything! The fact is that the pleasures in their lives do not offer the essential meaning they need and are seeking. Therefore, as they acquire more and more fifth and fourth class pleasure, they feel emptier and emptier, because they do not know how to get that which they truly crave.

If you have not found that conviction, if you have not lived for what you are willing to die for, then you have not really lived.

To really live, you need to tap into the pleasure of being good—it is a higher class.

Exercises~

❶ To what extent are you concerned with "looking good"? To what extent are you influenced by peer pressure? Consider the style of clothes you wear. Are they designer clothes? Do they represent the latest fashion?

❷ You get set up on a blind date. The person really is the nicest guy or gal you have ever dated. In fact, he or she is everything you ever dreamed of, except most people consider this person to be unattractive and the clothes he or she wears to be grossly out of style. You personally are physically attracted to this person, but your friends give you strange looks, and they have made comments, albeit indirectly. Are you influenced by their comments? Do you continue to see this person?

❸ Read the obituary column of your local newspaper. Who seems to have had the best life? Why? Write your own obituary column. How do you want to be remembered?

Second Class Pleasure: Getting Creative

Okay, maybe you can learn how to be good. Truly good. Now think about this: What is it that goodness cannot buy?

Second class pleasure is best identified by its counterfeit. What is the one thing that can drive a person to break all the rules, to sacrifice innocent lives? What is it that can drive an otherwise normal person to kill millions?

Power! The drive for power, or really its counterfeit, control, leads people to doing the most unimaginable things.

From Stalin to Idi Amin, Hitler, and Pol Pot, history contains a long list of tyrants willing to kill millions to get and maintain power, to be in control. The fact that people will forego any level of decency for a taste of this pleasure is evidence that it is weightier. This does not mean that one should forego materiality, love, and goodness, in order to attain power, for after all we are describing its counterfeit; but the fact that history contains countless examples of those who did so shows that we are now examining a whole new dimension of pleasure.

Still, control is only the counterfeit of the positive expression of power. Power in the *positive* sense is creativity. This is real power. This is the real pleasure that people are seeking.

> Second class pleasure is the power to create life, not destroy it. This real power is creativity.

The difference between third class pleasure and second class pleasure is the difference between a soldier and the general. The soldier knows he is part of the cause. He plays his role. The general sees much more. He shapes the overall campaign. He feels the responsibility for it. *Responsibility is the price one has to pay for second class pleasure.* The general is responsible for the outcome, which is a tremendous burden to carry. If successful, though, the general has a far greater reward.

> When the Soviet Union invaded Afghanistan in the 1980s, there was a doctor named Bob Simon, who was an associate professor of emergency medicine at UCLA.[3] Simon said to himself "I wonder who's providing medical care to the refugees inside Afghanistan." It turned out that most of the country's 1,500 physicians had been killed, imprisoned, or driven into exile and that organizations like Doctors Without Borders (a French group) were unable to respond effectively. So, Simon said to himself, "If no one else is doing anything, then it's my responsibility." He mortgaged his house and moved to Pakistan.
>
> He trained illiterate Afghani refugees how to be medics (how to extract bullets, splint broken bones, treat the dozen most common diseases) and sent them back across the border into Afghanistan. This was the primary medical care available in Afghanistan during the entire Russian occupation. Simon estimated that his trainees treated 50,000 patients per month. Imagine the pleasure of being able to look back at that achievement as your own—being the caregiver for an entire nation. As Simon himself says, "I'm lucky. Very few people in this world get the chance to really help other people when that help is critical."

[3] Kline, David. "Helping Hands: An L.A. Doctors Medical Corps. Struggles to Heal the Wounds of the Afghan War." *People Weekly*, vol. 29, May 16, 1988. pp 72-74.

The drive to be creative is an outgrowth of the recognition *that this is my world.* This recognition can cause a Dr. Simon to change his life; he sees an aspect of his world falling apart, so he must fix it. It is also what drives those who amass power to kill. Their motivation is to recreate the world to conform to their own imaginings, a communist state or a world dominated by the Aryan race. In the end, though, power used in this way destroys, as it is really egocentric and manipulative.

A necessary element of creativity is to have control over what you're creating. For example, the artist has to have control over his eye, his arm, and the paint, in order to translate an idea into reality. The artist must manipulate the raw material with which he is working. Therefore, people often make the mistake of thinking that simple manipulation makes them creative; they seek this control as an end in itself—and this is the counterfeit. Stalin, Hitler and Pol Pot were duped by this illusion. They manipulated, and thus, they destroyed lives and societies. In the end, they themselves fell, leaving nothing behind of their vision.

Real creativity is an expression of oneself outward into the world. Control is an attempt to restrict the outer world to comply with one's own self-centered vision of what reality should be. So, control is always to the detriment of others.

> The way to tell if you are creating or controlling is by the result: creativity gives pleasure to the creator and others, whereas control leads to destruction and misery.

Just as murder and destruction of societies are the lowest forms of power, which are the counterfeit of creativity, its highest expression is creating life. Just as life is the most sophisticated of all of creation, enhancing life and building upon it is the highest form of creativity. Giving pleasure to others and building them up, creating children and molding them to become good people, and affecting the positive growth of society are the highest forms of the second class of pleasure.

The true source of creative power is wisdom. In order to create you must first formulate a concept in your mind, which you desire to translate into reality. Thus, you must cultivate wisdom to become a connoisseur of creativity.

In other words, the second level of pleasure is to act wisely and by so doing bring pleasure to others in the world.

Exercises~

❶ Research the life of one of history's despots. What do you believe motivated this person?

❷ List a few of your heroes. Do you think that they share any common traits? Which ones? What you think motivated them to becoming the people that you admire?

❸ Imagine that you are President Truman in 1945. The war with Japan is dragging, and you have an atomic weapon at you disposal. Do you use it? Why or why not?

❹ Consider whether there is a connection between Mozart's ability to compose music and FDR's ability to craft the legislation that was to become the New Deal.

First Class Pleasure: Breaking Through

First class pleasure, the highest level of pleasure, is what every human being longs for.

Imagine you own a yacht, you have a home, money in the bank, you have a beautiful spouse, family, great friends, and you are an important doctor in the community, both in your practice and in various causes. You also teach at the local medical school, training the doctors in a revolutionary technique you developed to treat a particular disease. In a word, you have mastered each of levels of pleasure discussed so far.

You sit down and look over your life, and as satisfied and as meaningful as your life is, is it possible for you to sense that something is missing? With all this achievement, could you imagine having the feeling that you still do not have "*IT*"? What could that something be?

> Human beings have a drive for the ultimate experience. For many, it is a religious experience; for the surfer, it might be the ultimate wave. As seen throughout history and across cultural lines, the existence of this drive is indisputable.

To satisfy this need, many have searched romantically for the transcendental experience. For some this has been expressed in the pursuit for immortality, for the mystic waters of Eden. The great conquistador, Ponce de Leon, conquered much of America, searching for the spring of eternal life. The story of King Arthur is the story of the quest for the Holy Grail, for the cup that contains the drink of life. For the Hindu, the quest has been to reach a state of Nirvana.

> A California millionaire, Dennis Tito, paid $20 million, for the ultimate experience—a trip on a Russian rocket ship into outer space. One might have thought that Mr. Tito already had it all. He started his professional life as a rocket scientist for NASA engaged in groundbreaking work. Then he left the world of science to found an extremely successful investment-banking firm, which manages billions of dollars. He is blessed with three children. He owns one of the most fabulous houses in Los Angeles. He gives to politics and charities, and he sits on many boards. In a word, he is a man who has made it. Yet, all that was not enough; Mr. Tito needed to fulfill a dream and to touch the ultimate.

Ask any person you know: "Aren't you a little disappointed with what life has to offer? Aren't you hoping there's something more, that maybe one day you'll have an experience that will be *it*?" By and large the answer to these questions is "yes."

Each one of us deep down has a longing to reach out beyond ourselves, beyond our own finite world and to touch the infinite. Imagine if someone you trusted well told you, "I know a place where you can go and actually speak with God Himself. You can sit down and ask Him anything you like for an hour, and God will answer back." If we could actually have such an experience, would we all not agree that that would be the "*It*" experience?

No human being is totally satisfied unless he or she has fulfilled this spiritual need. We are all seeking to somehow sense the interconnectedness of all existence—to touch the transcendental.

The question now is whether this drive is for something real or for an illusion? The answer is for you to decide, *but it is incontrovertible that the drive exists.*

We have all had moments when we have been struck by the awesomeness of life, whether it was during the birth of a child, during a camping trip gazing up at the expansive star-lit sky, or during a beautiful sunset. We have all experienced something in life that takes our breath away. These moments were "awe" experiences.

The awe experience is where we sense our own beings merge somehow and to some degree with something greater then ourselves. It is the sense that we have broken through and beyond our limitations and touched the essence of existence. *This is first class pleasure.*

> First class pleasure is categorically above everything else—it is the drive for ultimate meaning, to sense who we are in the great scheme of things and to know that that place transcends the finite moment. This is the greatest of all pleasures.

Now, assuming for the moment that you agree that the drive for this pleasure is a drive for something real, as with everything else in life there would have to be a price. This being the greatest available pleasure, it must, of course, extract the greatest price (and it is *not* $20 million). That price is humility.

In order for you to transcend the finite and to see your place in the infinite scheme of things, you need to learn to be grateful for all the good that you now have. This is a very difficult awareness to attain, because the human ego always craves recognition and independence. Therefore, it has difficulty recognizing any source of benefit outside of itself.

However, by making the effort to recognize and appreciate all of the different good things that we have in life—health, friends, family—we can begin to be grateful. That gratefulness leads to humility. Humility allows us to be inspired by all of details of creation, from the beauty of something as simple as a piece of fruit to the expanse of the night sky, and this inspiration brings us to awe. To walk through life in a constant state of awe and wonderment, sensing a deep connection to all of reality is first class pleasure, a pleasure far and above any of the four categories below it.

The Counterfeit: Arrogance and Self-Absorption

There is of course a counterfeit of the first class experience: arrogance and self-absorption.

Just as humility will enable you to transcend your ego in order to perceive your greater self in the scheme of all of reality, its counterfeit promises to bring you to the same end. Arrogance and obsession with self create the illusion of the ultimate experience. To see oneself as all-powerful, in total control, and as king or queen of the world is a tremendous high. Indeed, this illusion can make it appear as though you're connecting to all of reality, because you're imagining that you encompass all of reality.

This is a high that seems complete. In truth, though, it is high that leaves no room for anything outside of yourself. As such, it leaves you with nowhere to truly transcend *to*. So, the experience is an illusion, which eventually crumbles.

Reaching for the Stars

Truly, these five levels of pleasure are interdependent: each builds on the other, and each level is necessary.

A single act can also provide the basis for any level of pleasure. A piece of fruit can be enjoyed simply for its own sake. It can also be given as a gift to someone you love. More than this, it can be taken to a homeless shelter and used to feed the poor. One can also take its seeds, and plant an orchard to feed a community. Finally, one can use it as a catalyst for sensing awe, as this one piece of fruit has such tremendous beauty and potential.

The five levels of pleasure are akin to the five stages that launch a rocket ship into orbit and send it to the moon. Fifth class physical pleasure gives us energy. We need good food, nice clothes, and a nice home. This is lift off. If we do not have fourth class pleasure, however, these amenities provide for a lonely existence without people to share them with. If we do not get married, have children, or have the love of brothers and sisters or friends, we will fall back to Earth. Everyone needs human contact. With love and friendship, we are traveling. Nonetheless, without third class pleasure, we will not make it into orbit. We will burn up in the Earth's atmosphere without self-respect, without satisfying our drive to be good people. Once in orbit, second-class pleasure propels us on our way. Creative power engendered by wisdom hurls us toward our destination. Having gone this far, though, we will never actually be able to land on the moon, if we do not allow ourselves to sense the awe of the trip we have taken.

Exercises~

❶ Have you ever had an awe experience? Describe what it was. What were the events leading up to this experience? Could you recreate them?

❷ Do you believe that the "awe" experience is something real, or is it an illusion? Explain?

❸ Assuming for the moment that the "awe" experience is something real, if one person states that they had such an experience watching a sunset (but this person hates the beach) and another person states that they had such an experience while surfing (but has never been impressed by a sunset), are they describing two different realities or two different paths to the same reality?

chapter 3

Mastering Your Free Will:
the Power *of* Choice

Now you know all about the Five Levels of Pleasure—or at least how they are defined. But how can you actually reach those higher levels of pleasure and start enjoying their benefits?

You now know that our primary motivation for just about everything is the drive for pleasure, and that not all pleasures are created equal, that there are various levels of pleasure available to a person, and these levels are qualitatively distinct one from the other. You also understand that the root of unhappiness and personal distress is the fact that human beings are prone to mistakes.

We often make errors in our judgment in choosing what pleasures to pursue. Of the options available to us, we will often choose one path thinking that it will lead us to our goal, whereas in reality, a different path would have led us to greater fulfillment. This problem is compounded by the fact that there exist counterfeit pleasures—experiences that promise the satisfaction we desire, but which in the end leave us feeling dissatisfied or even deflated.

As a result of our inclination to choose poorly, we can logically deduce that humanity could benefit from an education about life—an education about the types of pleasures available to a person and about how to choose effectively among these various options.

So, reaching the higher levels of pleasure is really all about informed decision making, and mastering a uniquely human trait called free will. You are now ready to delve into that process.

Choice and Free Will

The secret to accessing those higher levels of pleasure, informed decision making, only works when you accept the following assumption:

> People are capable of stepping out of themselves and their surroundings in such a way that they can make an independent judgment as to the correctness or incorrectness (some would say morality) of their actions.

Many philosophers would argue that this ability to step outside of oneself is what defines us as human beings. This ability is the distinguishing aspect of human consciousness, and it allows humans to define their own existence. Philosopher René Descartes' statement, "I think, therefore I am," epitomizes this understanding: *I am a conscious being; therefore, I can establish my own existence.*

Let's take a step back and to look at the larger issue of the nature of the human condition.

No one can dispute that in all of creation—human beings are unique. Humanity has tremendous power and potential and has exhibited this in opposite extremes: On the one hand, humanity has used its intellect to gain mastery over much of the physical world—from building spanning bridges to erecting enormous skyscrapers to harnessing atomic energy. On the other hand, human passion has caused tremendous misery, has led to the extinction of a plethora of other species, and, if unleashed, could destroy the entire world.

Indeed, the human can be more dangerous than the most vicious of animals; and yet, there is no creature that can match the human in its capacity for kindness and creativity.

Indeed, there seems to be a great dichotomy in the nature of being human. The question is why is this so. Is there some aspect of being human, some character trait, that more than any other distinguishes humans and accounts for this dichotomy?

We previously acknowledged that human beings have the capacity to define themselves and their own destiny in a way distinct from all other creatures and that this results from human consciousness. The issue to explore is whether there is something more specific that we can identify within this consciousness that explains why human action is expressed in such opposite extremes, both on a personal and societal level.

Surely, the answer to the question is something called free will. Free will is the human character trait that allows for this vast array of expressive behavior. It is free will that distinguishes human consciousness from that of animals.

To demonstrate the truth of this assertion and to understand its implications, we need to clearly define free will. We must also first define the concept of freedom.

Freedom cannot simply mean a lack of physical constraints. After all, you can live in America with all the money in the world and all the potential to be and become anything, and at the same time, be so trapped by your own past and own individual circumstances that all of this potential is squandered. You need only look at the wasted lives of so many of the rich and famous to know that this is true.

On the other hand, you can be in prison or living under dictatorial rule, and yet be so in control of your own thoughts and your own drives that the physical constraints only act as a catalyst enabling you to realize your potential as a human being. The names Mandela, Sokharov, and even Tookie Williams—a former California gang member executed in 2005 for a multiple murder, and at the same time nominated for the Nobel Peace Prize for anti-gangs efforts while in prison—prove this to be true.

> Clearly, the challenge of life cannot be seen in terms of your ability to control your physical environment. Instead, the challenge needs to be framed in terms of your response to the environment in which you find yourself.

You are free to the extent that you have options and recognize them. The challenge of freedom is for you to see and exploit these options. *Freedom, therefore, is a factor of your ability to choose.* But is every choice an expression of your free will, or does the "will" component imply a limitation of sorts?

Is free will simply the ability to exercise preferences? If you decide to enter a restaurant and the menu has the option of steak or chicken, and you decide on chicken—was this decision an exercise of your free will? If so, what makes humanity unique? Even animals have the ability to express preferences. A dog, for example, will drink filtered water as opposed to tap water if given the choice.

The answer must be "no"—deciding on chicken is not an expression of your free will. It is picking. You picked chicken because over time the synapses in your brain built-up an experiential relationship with chicken that it was more favorable than beef, so you picked chicken. Obviously, picking chicken over meat cannot be seen as a deep expression of your humanity. We make these types of decisions every day, but they do not define us; they do not cause us to grow. We cannot look at them and gain any deep insight into who we are. Therefore, free will must be something more profound.

Since freedom relates to our ability to choose, but not every choice is a manifestation of our free will, then *free will must be a type of choice.*

Good vs. Evil

In trying to define what types of choices are expressions of our free will, some might conclude that free will is a choice between good and evil. Would you agree?

Let us analyze this premise. Does not everyone try to choose good, albeit imperfectly? Does anyone choose to be bad or evil? Does anyone wake up in the morning thinking, "What tremendous evil can I do today?"

Every human being wants to be good, wants to use his or her potential, wants to do the right thing, wants accomplishment, wants meaning. Even the people we consider to be the most wicked, underneath it all, want to be good. This is why everyone rationalizes their behavior to define it as good. Stalin wanted to create the ideal state, and so did Hitler. They rationalized that the evil they caused was necessary to achieve the ultimate good. In their own minds, even the greatest of despots considered their actions to be "good."

As a result, free will choices cannot be understood in terms of the conflict between good and evil. Since we are all seeking the good, defining free will in terms of good and evil would leave us with no real choice. Only one real option would exist, and we would not really be choosing between anything. Effective choice would be a matter of accurate perception. Ineffective choice would simply be mistaken reactions to externally defined stimuli leading to an evil end. Personal growth would have little to do with how we grow as people, but rather how proficient we become at predicting the ultimate effect of our actions, or how lucky we are, since we are all intending toward the same result. We obviously need a different criterion.

The Freudian school of psychoanalysis suggests that the human psyche has two basic drives—one toward life (which includes the libidinal drive and the instinct toward self-preservation) and another toward death—a death instinct or death wish.[1] If this proposition is true, all human impulses are a manifestation of one of these two drives. Such a defining point provides a basis for understanding the nature of free will choices and for distinguishing them from other types of decisions. In essence, a free will choice becomes one, which implicates this fundamental struggle between life and death. Our "will" is the factor that determines how the struggle is resolved.

Life vs. Death

At first glance, defining free will in terms of a choice between life and death appears perplexing. After all, we all want to live. Survival seems to be our predominant instinct. The average person does not seriously consider suicide—certainly not on a regular, or even on a semi-regular basis. However, when we delve deeper into the concept of a death choice the connection becomes clear.

---

[1] See *Suggested Readings* for Chapter 3 in the Appendix.

In order to gain this clarity, we need to analyze the ultimate "death" decision: suicide. We need to consider what a person is choosing when he or she chooses to die. We need to consider this person's motivation. When someone picks up a gun or takes an overdose of pills in order to end it all, he or she is obviously suffering from tremendous pain. The stress and strain on such a person is beyond our comprehension. Nonetheless, equally obvious is the fact that the action is motivated by a desire to escape, to find an immediate and total cessation of pain.

> Imagine a man about to jump off the Brooklyn Bridge. You are the police psychologist sent to talk to him. He tells you that he is suffering from a terminal illness and is in near constant pain. As a result of the cost of treatment, he is now destitute, having wasted over a million dollars on useless treatments. His house is in foreclosure. His wife is leaving him and is having an affair. His children have not spoken to him for years, and none of them ever gave him any pleasure. His former business partners are suing him for a breach of trust and actions, which if guilty, would subject him to criminal prosecution. You tell the man to wait. You call the station and confirm the man's whole story.

What do you do? Should you let him jump, or do you talk him down? What is the man's motivation to jump? What could you say to talk the man down?

Suicide is an option when a person focuses on the pain of living. If you cannot give this person a reason to deal with that pain, or some type of hope or purpose for living; if you cannot help him refocus, than he might as well jump. Suicide is an escape. It is taking the easy way out to avoid the pain and effort of living. To talk the man down, you have to give him meaning. He needs to see that his suffering is worthwhile, that it is purposeful.

Victor Frankl, author of the book *Man's Search for Meaning*[2] and founder of logotherapy, sometimes referred to as the Third School of Psychoanalysis, asserts that the primary cause of mental illness is a lack of meaning. Logotherapy states that to cure people of their

---

[2] Frankl, Victor E. *Man's Search for Meaning.* Washington Square Press (New York, 1984).

mental illnesses, you need to help them find meaning in their lives so that life for them becomes worthwhile.

This is the death choice: In life, there is always a pull to run away—to give up. We could quit at any moment of the day. At its core, free will is the choice between this drive and the effort necessary to confront life's challenges and make them meaningful.

Right now we are making life-and-death free will choices—we are all deciding at this very moment whether to take the pain of growing, or to quit for the day and put off living until tomorrow.

People can choose death by committing suicide. There are also subtler ways to choose death. Taking drugs is another way of removing oneself from reality. One can also choose a slow death by killing time. When someone turns on the television and tunes out, because of boredom, he or she in a sense commits suicide for those moments. The average school child watches between 1,200 to 1,800 hours of television a year.[3] That is almost as much time as the average person works in a year. Imagine what could be accomplished with these lives were a life choice to be made instead!

Free will is the choice to live or to run away from life, which is in effect to die.

When we look to escape our problems, we escape being great. Now and then we all choose to escape from the effort necessary to accomplish our goals and ambitions. Deep down we all want to be great; we all want to change the world. However, we do not always feel like putting in the effort. So, we distract ourselves and escape from who we really are and what we want to achieve.

> Every moment we are alive, we are using our free will to choose between life and death. Whether we are aware of it or not, we are in constant conflict between these two choices. How we resolve that conflict is where our greatness lies. Our greatness is found in using our free will to live, fight and accomplish—rather than to quit and run away. This is growth. This is life's battle.

---

[3] The Ethics Resource Center. "Making the Case for Character Education, Environmental Factors, Media Images." http://www.ethics.org/character/media.html.

Free will gives each of us enormous power and potential. As potentially powerful as free will is, though, it is greatly underutilized. Generally, people are unaware that they have this power, so they cannot take advantage of it. Learning how to employ this power is the object of this chapter. In this process, we will learn that there are five stages to actualizing one's free will, and at each stage, there are relatively simple strategies for success. However, making them part of our lives takes a lot of practice.

Exercises~

❶ Evaluate the explanation of free will that I just presented to you. Do you agree that the fundamental constituent of free will is choosing life over death? Critique this idea.

❷ Understanding the notion of free will has been one of the central problems of philosophy for thousands of years. In this discussion, there are two primary schools of thought: One is the notion of determinism ("whether concepts related to human actions name events which result wholly from antecedent causal chains of the sort described by physical science"[4]) and the second is the notion of moral responsibility. The issue is whether human actions are in some way predetermined or can a person be held morally responsible for their actions. How do you feel about these differing views? What do your friends think?

[4] Edwards, P., ed. *The Encyclopedia of Philosophy,* vol 2. MacMillan (New York. 1967). p. 104.

Stage One: Awareness

Right this very second you are making a decision—whether to continue reading this book or to stop. You may be thinking: "Do I really care about this subject of free will? I wish I was watching television." Or, you may be thinking, "This is interesting and important. I must pay attention." Whichever alternative you choose, you will be making a choice. The only issue is whether you are consciously aware of making that choice.

Life is a never-ending stream of choices; making choices is a constant. The first stage of mastering free will is becoming aware that you are making choices all the time. Do not let yourself be swept along by some tide of action or feeling over which you have no control!

Have you ever had the experience of getting into your car, turning on the engine, and then ending up at your destination without any recollection of the turns that you made along the way? This is a common experience. People can have no memory of a 20 to 30 minute trip. Yet, during that time they made literally hundreds of decisions, some even critically important—when to speed up, when to slow down, what to look at, when turn, when to yield to a pedestrian. All this and the entire time is a blank in the driver's mind. What a scary thought!

A common criticism of organized religions is that they often seem to be obsessed with a system of ritual that encourages doing things by rote, without thought and consideration, and, therefore, without meaning. Yet, many of us live our lives without much thought; we go about our daily chores and routines by rote.

Don't make your life one big blank! Become aware! You decide! Once you become sensitive to this phenomenon, you can begin to monitor and examine your choices.

In some religions there is an idea that when one passes from this world to the next, judgment will consist of a minute by minute recounting of one's life. From this perspective, a full life is one in which each moment can be *positively* accounted for.

Indeed, a full life, a life which has mastered its free will, is one full of memories. In sum total, we are nothing but a composite of the memories that we carry with us. Our memories make up who we are. They define us.

> You come to this moment with a picture in your mind of the person you are, and that picture is nothing but the result of the memories and the interpretation of these memories that you hold in your mind.

In fact, the bigger a person is, so to speak, the more memories and a greater a life of worthwhile moments he or she will experience. It is no coincidence that by and large, great historical figures, great leaders, generally share the common trait of keeping a journal or writing memoirs. A remarkable fact of history is that even though President Nixon's taping of Whitehouse conversations cost him his job during the Watergate scandal, every subsequent president has maintained this same practice. Important people realize that each of their moments is too precious to be lost in the sea of time.

If you want to gain an appreciation for the truth of this point and for the power of memory to expand your own life, try keeping a journal for one month. At the end of each day, record five significant events. By doing this, you will see that your days become bigger and your weeks more significant. At the end of a month, you will be a bigger person, because you will have more of yourself to carry with you.

Effective use of free will requires *conscious behavior*—an awareness that each moment counts. Each moment presents a new option for thoughtful decision-making.

Complacency is the enemy of free will. If you are merely ambivalent about life, not really caring about the events happening around you, with no desire to get involved, then you are casting your free will to the wind. If you're like this, then you are drifting with the tide of life.

Don't let your decisions just happen! Take control! Constantly ask yourself: "Is this the decision that I want to make?" Your decisions shape your life. Awareness is the first step to accessing your free will. By getting on top of your decisions, you take charge of your destiny.

Exercises~

❶ How many decisions have you made since you got up today? Try to list them (What color of shirt to wear? Have one doughnut or two? Stop the car and let those pedestrians pass? Whom do I sit beside in class?) To what extent did you consider each decision? To what extent did each decision matter to your life? What forces influenced these decisions—someone else's opinion, habit, other external circumstances?

❷ For a month, keep a journal in which you record at the end of each day five important events. Consider after one month whether this exercise changed you? Are you more alive now then before you kept the journal?

❸ Watch the movie *BladeRunner*. What distinguishes human beings from replicants that justified replicants being eliminated? Memories were inserted into the minds of certain replicants. What role did these memories play in the creation of their personalities? Is this realistic?

Stage Two: Independence

The second stage of mastering free will is independence. Independence is made up of three components:

* ✳ Not being constrained by preconceptions
* ✳ Self-knowledge
* ✳ Responsibility

Preconceptions

There are two types of preconceptions: externally defined and internally defined.

Externally defined preconceptions can constrain you when you allow someone else's view of you to control your decisions. When you act a certain way, consciously or unconsciously, in order to live up to another's expectations, or in order to comply with another view of who you are, you are minimizing your free will. Hey…we're all too easily led by peer pressure and the values defined by our society. These external factors limit our actions. Surmounting these obstacles is difficult and requires independence.

> To appreciate how easily people can be controlled by external preconceptions, consider the true story of Jeff's job interview. Jeff had worked a couple years of for a small law firm in the field of securities transactions but professionally felt dissatisfied. Jeff thought perhaps he would be happier working on the business-side of a deal, so he arranged for an interview with a major investment bank.
>
> During the interview, the interviewer looked at Jeff's resume and back at Jeff, and then again he looked at the resume and back at Jeff. Finally, after a few moments, the interviewer said, "You know when people come to work for us, they generally have the same-type of focused background. In university, they major in business, they do an internship with an investment bank, and afterward they pursue an MBA. You, on the other hand, when I look at your resume, I see that you have been all over the place." In short, this man was calling Jeff a flake!
>
> Now, Jeff had always tried to make relatively conservative decisions; in fact, he was the straight arrow in his family. Nonetheless, he did have a varied background. In reaction to his interviewer's statement, Jeff was seized by an immediate sense of depression and felt trapped by his non-conventional past. His self-confidence plummeted—all because he let someone else control his view of himself. Had Jeff been more independent, Jeff could have responded, "It's a very good thing that I've had these different experiences. Through them I have become well

rounded. I know some of what life has to offer, and I know what I want now."

Just as people allow others to define them, so also do people often become prisoners of themselves. An internally defined preconceived notion is a view of oneself defined in the past. When you view life and its options today simply because that is the view developed yesterday, you're limiting yourself. When you make a decision based on yesterday, you often refuse to reevaluate *today* solely out of pride and stubbornness. When you do that you're giving up part of your independence.

You must develop a constant willingness to look at life afresh in order to be sure that what was chosen in the past continues to be the optimal decision today. You must always be willing to gather new evidence and make a more informed decision. *Start each day anew!*

Self-Knowledge

Did you ever notice that two people can look at the exact same event and see two opposite realities. For example, in conflicts, like those in Northern Ireland or the Middle East, in each camp, there are always two groups: the doves and the hawks. After a terrorist attack, the doves always cry, "Don't you see, more than ever this is exactly why we need a peace-process. You hawks are part of the problem. We need to end this conflict now!" On the other side, the hawks cry, "Don't you see, this is exactly why we can't have peace. Those other people, they are animals. If we give in, it will be more of the same!" Each side wants so desperately to see itself as right that it subconsciously colors events to reflect its desires.

We are all looking for confirmation in the world of what we believe to be true in our hearts. When we hear or see something we do not like, we selectively block out the message or we interpret it in a perverse way so that it fits into our worldview. This results from the fact that people are generally unable to simultaneously maintain in their mind two contradictory thoughts. This phenomenon is termed cognitive dissonance.

To escape this trap and free yourself to think independently requires self-knowledge. Self-knowledge empowers you to evaluate whether you are interpreting events accurately or whether you're fooling yourself into believing that reality is something that its not. Self-knowledge enables you to ensure that you are guiding the decision-making and not the decisions guiding you!

Responsibility

Independence also implies that you can take complete responsibility for your own actions. No one makes your choices for you, and no one is responsible for the outcome except for you, the decision-maker. Your success or failure is in your own hands. This is the attitude of any really successful person.

> Christopher Osakwe exemplifies the responsible person. Mr. Osakwe was the lead negotiator for a major US soft-drink company and a multinational fast-food restaurant when those companies first entered the market of the former Soviet Union. Both deals pioneered the entry of American companies into the then-communist state. At the time, Mr. Osakwe was one of perhaps five Western attorneys licensed to practice law in both the U.S. and Russia. An interesting fact about Mr. Osakwe is that he is a person of color and that he received his legal training in Moscow at a time when other people of color from African nations suffered severe prejudice. Mr. Osakwe was once asked whether he had ever had a problem being black, either while studying in the former Soviet Union or in his climb up the predominantly white old-boy network of American law firms. His response was simply to look at the questioner as if he were crazy to ask such a question. For Mr. Osakwe, being a person of color was a given circumstance; whereas, his success or failure was a function of his own choices.

Having the attitude where you accept total responsibility for your own life is a very high level to aspire to. For many of us, it is all too easy to blame our circumstances and others for our lack of success.

The story of Tzvi exemplifies this. Tzvi was a budding lead gui-
tarist. He and his drummer roommate were on the fast track to
nowhere, when they decided that they had to do something to
jump-start their careers. They agreed to go to open band night at
local bars, where house bands allow people from the audience to
play with them. This would be the path to their being discov-
ered. The problem was that, generally, house bands only choose
people from the audience who they knew could play.

After all, house bands did not want some novice ruining
everyone's evening. New faces were only invited on stage a half-
hour or so before closing, if at all. When a couple of weeks past
without getting a chance to play, Tzvi gave up. His drummer
friend, however, continued going until he was chosen a few
times. That was all he needed. House bands began to recognize
his talents. So, when one of the regular drummers got sick, he
was asked to sit in. From there he got offers to do other gigs.
Meanwhile, Tzvi continued moping at home. He complained
about how unfair life was; and when he saw his friend succeed-
ing, nothing his friend could do was right—he was a slob; he
played his music too loud; he used up all the hot water. Tzvi
readily admits today that was a low point in his life, because he
was blaming everyone else for his predicament except himself.

At the end of the day, we rise or fall solely as a result of our own
choices in the face of the obstacles in our path. The responsibility of
independence is having the courage to recognize this fact.

Independence demands opening your mind to see clearly the
world around you. It requires having the self-knowledge to under-
stand how our internal desires color our picture of the world. It also
necessitates the fortitude to take responsibility for the place in which
we find ourselves. With independence, even when external circum-
stances are beyond your control, you can choose your attitude and
your values.

Exercises~

❶ In deciding to attend a university and in deciding which university to attend, how influential were your parents in determining the outcome?

❷ If you are a student, who is responsible for your tuition payments? Is your independence compromised because you are financially beholden to someone else?

❸ Do people consider you smart, good-looking, creative, stylish? To what effect does another's view of you impact on your behavior? Do you care what others think? Is it ever important what others think of you?

❹ Chose a hot current political subject and read two commentaries from opposite perspectives on the issue. To what extent do you feel that the commentators are agreed on the underlying factual issues? Do they seem to be describing the same reality?

❺ Read William Ernest Henley's poem "Invictus," found on the next page, and think about what must be the author's concept of independence and responsibility. Does the poem reflect your attitude toward life?

Stage Three: Understanding Body and Soul

The greater the proportion of your actions that arise out of *conscious choice,* and the greater the degree to which you are prepared to be independent, the more effective you will be as a human being.

The third stage to actualizing your free will involves recognizing that within the human condition exists a fundamental struggle,

Invictus
by William Ernest Henly

Out of the night that covers me,
Black as the Pit from pole to pole,
I thank whatever gods there be
For my unconquerable soul.

In the fell clutch of circumstance
I have not winced nor cried aloud.
Under the bludgeoning of chance
My head is bloody, but unbowed.

Beyond this place of wrath and tears
Looms but the horror of the shade,
And yet the menace of the years
Finds, and shall find, me unafraid.

It matters not how strait the gate,
How charged with punishment the scroll,
I am the master of my fate:
I am the captain of my soul.

which for the lack of a better descriptor we will refer to as *the body and the soul conflict*.

Within the consciousness of every culture is some permutation of the body-soul conflict. This concept is dealt with in both religion and philosophy. Both find the metaphor to be an apt descriptor of the human condition. Indeed, so pervasive is the idea that society seems to take its existence for granted.

It is a common theme in books and movies. Even Fred Flintstone has struggled with the conflict. In some episodes of the Flintstones, Fred faces moral dilemmas. In these situations, a little devil Fred Flintstone pops up on one side of Fred's head decked out in the complete garb including horns and a pointy tail, while opposite the little devil appears a miniature angelic Fred dressed in white with a halo and wings. Our hero's dilemmas are resolved after the two little Freddys fight it out.

The issue to address is whether this theme is rooted in reality or whether it is just fanciful make believe.

You cannot deny that every human being experiences an internal struggle between physical desires and noble aspirations. A few moments of contemplation reveal that we all share common experiences, which confirm some type of internal body and soul conflict. You need only remember that last time you tried to initiate a diet or begin an exercise routine. Perhaps you attempted to take up jogging, and early in the morning on the first day, an hour before you would ordinarily have woken up from a cozy bed, your body whispered, "This is ridiculous, sleep in just today." The soul responds, "But I am so out of shape, I have to do something." Then, if you are actually able to make it out of bed and start toward the door, the body argues, "Ahg! It's too cold outside. Let's wait a few days until the weather gets a bit warmer. Think harder there has to be a simpler way to get in shape." And still your wiser half fights on, "You will feel so much better afterward; you'll be healthier, more vital, and live longer." It seems that we are all just a little schizophrenic!

The same kinds of struggles take place in all areas of life, from exploring issues of personal growth to tackling difficult ethical decisions. At the end of the day, the soul says, "let's start a journal," while the body says, "you don't need to sit down right now; wait until morning." Or, when deciding whether to take some office supplies home from work, your body might argue, "its OK to take those pens home, your boss expects employees to take a few." Meanwhile, the soul queries, "Isn't this stealing?" Late at night, while writing the next day's assignment, a student may begin to experience hunger pangs. Obviously, the student needs to eat and might think, "I think I need a Snickers to tide me over," whereupon he or she gets up and heads for the store. Consider what is happening. How real is the hunger? Is it just an excuse for procrastination?

In philosophy, there is a great debate about whether the body and soul are two completely separate and distinct entities, or whether both are really one and the same thing.[5] In either event, however, the whole debate comes because there is a universal recognition of a dichotomy, which exists and demands explanation.

If we can agree that inside each of us is some type of internal conflict, then we must strive for a deeper understanding of the nature of the soul.

> For our purposes, it is sufficient to say that the soul is simply that image of ourselves, which represents the person we truly want to be. Our soul is our drive to reach our potential and to attain something beyond ourselves. Our soul is that part of ourselves which strives for meaning, clarity and purpose. The soul seeks to grow, to tackle challenges, and to overcome obstacles. Essentially, the soul seeks life.

The body by definition is physical. This is not to suggest that physicality is negative. However, the body is that part of ourselves which seeks transitory comfort and sensual pleasures in manner disassociated from anything beyond the present moment. The body yearns for a pain-free existence; it wants to drown in passions, to procrastinate, and to quit.

Thus, these two aspects of who we are push in opposite directions, essentially one pushes toward life and the other towards death.

At the outset of this chapter, we demonstrated that a free will choice at its core is a decision between life and death. If this is true, the body and soul conflict holds the key to discovering how to make effective life choices.

Learning to recognize the conflict and to distinguish between the cravings of the body and the aspirations of the soul are imperative to

---

[5] See the *Suggested Readings* for Chapter 3 in the Appendix.

actualizing your free will. In the end, as you shall see, success in this struggle is about self-mastery.

An old fable aptly describes the battle between body and soul as the battle of conquering yourself:

> A group of soldiers was returning home after winning a war. As they are marching and singing, flushed with victory, an old man comes out to greet them on the road. He says to them:
>
> "Friends, you think you have achieved a major victory, but the truth is you merely won a very minor battle. It is only now that you will confront a major war—the war within yourselves. When you fight a human enemy and win, you have peace—at least temporarily, until he regroups. In the internal war, even when you've just won the battle, the enemy is after you again immediately. When you fight a human enemy and are defeated, you can usually run away. Your opponent may chase you for a day or two, but if you run far enough, he will get tired and stop coming after you. In the internal war, no matter how far you run, the enemy will keep coming after you."

When you fight a human enemy and he breaches your camp, you know you are in real trouble. You do everything in your power to prevent that from happening. In the internal battle, the enemy has no need to breach the camp because he is already there. He is you.

Indeed, who is the truly mighty person? Is it the physically strong—the Arnold Schwarzenegger? Even a muscle man can fall from a bullet or virus. Is it the wise man? There will always be someone to come along after and dispute the wise man's ideas.

In the words of Thomas Hobbes, "Nature has made men so equal in the faculties of the body and mind as that, though there be found one man sometimes manifestly stronger in body or of quicker mind than another, yet, when all is reckoned together, the difference between man and man is not so considerable as that one man can thereupon claim to himself any benefit to which another may not pretend as well as he. For as to the strength of body, the weakest has

---

[6] Hobbes, Thomas. *The Leviathan.* Tuck, Richard, ed. Cambridge University Press (Cambridge, 1996).

strength enough to kill the strongest, either by secret machination or by confederacy with others...."[6]

Surely then, the only true test of strength is the degree to which you can master *yourself*. After all, the self is the only thing that you have complete dominion over!

Exercises~

❶ Do you think that the body and soul always be in conflict? Can there be harmony between body and soul? If so, under what conditions?

❷ Jot down several personal examples, such as the jogging, where you have experienced a conflict between body and soul.

❸ Write a page about one dream that you would like to accomplish in your lifetime. What things within yourself are holding you back?

❹ What is the real you? Is it the body? (What if a someone losses an arm or has a heart transplant?) Is it the mind? (But what if someone loses their memory and suffers from dementia?) Is it moral consciousness? (But what if in an uncontrollable fit of anger or depression, one person kills another?) What is the essential you?

Stage Four: Growth

The body-soul conflict is the internal struggle that we all face. It is essentially a struggle between life and death, between growth and complacency. It is a struggle between our physical desire for comfort and our noble desire to exert effort to achieve. The key to self-mastery and the road to self-perfection lie in how we resolve this conflict. An approach to this end may be termed *Identifying with the Soul.*

> Identifying with the Soul is learning to follow the direction of soul in making free will choices. Since the soul is the greater vision of yourself that we hold in your mind's eye, the soul represents the real you. It is the person you have the potential to become.

Therefore, the soul is that aspect of yourself that pushes you. In spite of this drive, however, when you do not realize that inside of yourself is this dichotomy of body and soul, you can easily find yourself on a road to self-impairment. Without this awareness, you can easily be tempted to follow the lead of your body down a path of escapism and stagnation, brought about by pursuing creature comforts. For example, when a your body says, "I'm hungry," you can easily be tempted to stop what you are doing to run out and get a Snickers bar, even when waiting would be a wiser course of action.

Again, this observation is not meant to denigrate the body. To the contrary, you must keep yourself fit and of course you need to enjoy physical pleasures. Nevertheless, by identifying with the soul as opposed to the body, you have the capability of reaching toward self-perfection!

One way to begin the process of identifying with the soul is by using empowering speech. Do not say, *"I am* thirsty." Rather, say, *"My body* needs some water." Do not say, *"I am* tired." Instead say, *"My body* needs sleep." Then, you can evaluate whether the needs of your body, which it truly feels, override other concerns of the moment.

The challenge of identifying with your soul is really a matter of training your body to *reflect the desires* of your soul. This training process begins when you learn to be sensitive to the point where your choices are actually a manifestation of your free will.

However, the point where your decisions are a manifestation of your free will is different for each individual. *Everyone has a unique free will point.* For example, for most people, murder is not an option. If handed a gun, the decision not to kill an innocent bystander is not a free will choice. It is a given. Similarly, you could argue that most people do not seriously consider stealing to be an option. However, many will take office pens and other office supplies home with them for personal use. Others pilfer hotel towels or ashtrays as vacation souvenirs. And believe it or not, restaurants report that people frequently pocket table flatware! These actions are stealing, but some people justify such behavior as an acceptable social norm.

So it is obvious that the issue of stealing is not so clear for everyone. For a great many of us, to steal or not to steal in these kinds of circumstances is a real moral dilemma. We have not worked on ourselves to such a degree that not taking these items without explicit permission has become a non-option. This is where our free will lies, and each of us resolves such dilemmas in our own unique fashion.

Training our bodies to reflect our souls requires becoming sensitive to our points of real conflict and then working to raise these points of our free will, in a sense our personal moral standards, to higher and higher levels. You can raise your point of free will by assisting the soul to employ a counter-strategy to the drives of the body. This works by understanding how your body operates and teaching your soul to function in the same way.

When faced with a moral dilemma or challenge of personal growth, most people do not generally intend to do the wrong thing, at least not directly. They tend to justify their actions, allowing their bodies to mislead them into acting in a less appropriate way. For instance, having made the decision to diet, when a friend tempts the dieter with a mouth-watering piece of chocolate cream pie, the dieter's immediate reaction will be, "No. I shouldn't. I'm trying to lose weight." The body functions subtly to persuade the dieter otherwise. The body says, "Just a little bite, that can't hurt," or, "This is the last piece of pie you'll have, and tomorrow you'll begin the diet in full."

You have to appreciate what is happening. Having committed yourself to dieting, your body would never argue, "Oh, just forget the diet. It's okay to be fat. Have the pie." After all, you are not *really* schizophrenic. The body and soul are both a part of you, the single person that you are. The body simply houses your drive in the alternative direction; but it is still a part of you. The body will not take a tack in complete disregard of who you are.

Therefore, as a dieter you know, *and your body knows*, that abandoning the diet outright at the first temptation will not happen. Instead, the pull of body exists at the point of free will, at the point where there is the greatest lack of clarity. The pull of the body is to convince you to give in just a tiny bit, yet still believe that you are in control. So, your body says something like, "Let me have just a little piece; it won't effect my calorie count *that* much." Recognize though, that once you give in a little bit, it becomes harder to resist next time, and after that the diet is over.

The counter strategy of the soul must be the same. Succeeding in any plan of personal growth requires you to coax yourself into action. For example, to initiate and maintain an exercise routine, you cannot say to yourself on the first day, "From now on, every morning, fifty pushups and a five mile run." Such an approach is almost doomed to failure. You simply may be nowhere near that level of action; it is not who you are.

Instead, *you need to grow into the person you want to become.* A more effective approach might be: "For the next fifteen minutes, I'll exercise—some push-ups, stretching, and jogging in place. Afterward, I'll reward myself with some chocolate cake." Similarly, at the end of the day, when you are tired but want to do something worthwhile instead of killing time in front of the TV, you might say to your body, "Come on, let's study for just half an hour. Then we'll go watch TV." You have to stage the battle at your point of free will.

Fortunately, when you use this strategy, the body learns to follow along with the aspirations of the soul. As you gain control over your body, little by little, the body learns to appreciate what the soul wants. This is how you raise your point of free will.

Think again about the first time a person gets out of bed early to go jogging. The struggle is so painful. Yet, by the tenth time, it is generally much easier. By the hundredth time, the jogger does not seriously consider *not* getting up.

The same approach works in all aspects of life. If you were to decide to become a vegetarian, in the first few weeks your mouth might still water when you see and smell a roast coming out of the oven. A year later, the thought of meat in any form may just make you nauseous.

Learning to identify with your soul molds your body to become a reflection of your soul. It raises your point of free will and develops the self. This is stage four of mastering free will.

Exercises~

❶ Devise, execute, and record the results of a self-modification project, whereby you apply behavior modification methods to positively change an aspect of your personal character.

❷ Identify a goal that you have had for a long time, but you have been unsuccessful in making headway to achieve. Can you apply the principles of this section of the book to making a plan to achieve this goal?

Stage Five: Direction

On its most basic level free will requires an awareness that you have options. To fully take advantage of these options, you need to be independent. On another level, effective decision-making requires that you are aware of the body-soul conflict and that you engage in a process of identifying with the soul. This process results in raising your point of free will. Viewed another way, this process results in raising the moral and ethical standards by which you actually live.

In other words, mastering your free will is the key to self-growth and reaching your full potential or fulfillment and success!

No person can exist in a static state of being; your point of free will is constantly in flux. Given how difficult change and growth are, as difficult as it is for you to raise your point of free will, you can easily slip back into bad habits and old patterns of behavior. Therefore, you must choose to grow.

> **Growth is a free will choice to exert the constant effort necessary to increasing your free will point.**

Throughout this process of mastering your free will, even though increased awareness and independence may free you from living your life by rote, to a large extent you may *still* make decisions throughout the day out of habit. However, these habits of behavior are chosen ones; they are habits that will increasingly reflect conscious choice. In essence, as a free will master, you will take control of an inevitable process which otherwise would be directed by the subconscious.

When you choose growth constantly, you raise your vision to greater sights and bigger challenges. Personal development is thus a natural consequence of identifying with the soul.

The final stage of free will is to take control of this process and direct it. This requires formulating a clear picture in your mind of the person you ultimately want to be, and committing yourself to invest the effort to become this person. The final stage of free will requires that you eagerly accept the challenge of always working to refine your character, as well as a willingness always to be open and ready to learn, to correct mistakes, and to seek new ways to reach ever higher ideals.

The final stage connects the self to *beyond self*. Whether your ideal is to become a great businessperson, a great statesman, a great teacher, a great academic, a great homemaker, or any other endeavor, greatness demands a connection with and influence over others and the world around you. Therefore, when you place in your mind a picture of greatness, you also must necessarily create a picture of how you desire to connect and interact with your environment. This connection then is the drive of the soul, and through your free will you can achieve it!

As we discussed earlier in this chapter, the conflict between the body and soul is really a conflict between life and death. The body wants to rest, to sleep, to die, while the soul desires to live and to reach beyond itself. Honing and exercising your free will to learn and grow, to achieve high ideals, will enable you to change the world—your personal world, and the larger one too.

Committing yourself to growth, and through that growth process expanding and reaching beyond the "self" to contribute to the health and happiness of others through your choices—that's how you can change the world for the better and tap into your full potential.

Exercises~

❶ In what field do you think you'd like to achieve greatness? Make a list of the defining attributes that would qualify a person as great in that field. Devise a plan to inculcate yourself to represent one of those traits.

❷ In this book we've asserted that a person must attempt to exist in a state of constant awareness, and we've also discussed a process of habit formation. Do these ideas contradict each other? Are we presenting inconsistent ideas?

chapter 4

Using Your Intellect
to Achieve Pleasure

Are you smarter than average? Do you consider yourself to be an intellectual?

What is an intellectual? Does it have something to do with a high IQ? And why should you care?

People these days often define an intellectual as someone who is lost in a world of thought; —an impractical, hair-splitting, absent-minded professor. However, the opposite is true. And harnessing your intellectual abilities is the key to pleasure.

The intellect is the power of knowing, as distinguished from the power of feeling. Intellectuals use their minds, rather than their feelings, to guide themselves through life. They lead with the head, not the heart.

Having intelligence doesn't make you an intellectual. You can be brilliant but still let your feelings rule your life. True intellectuals use *understanding* to arrive at reality, regardless of their intelligence.

This chapter will show you how to become an intellectual, and explain why this is key to effective living, reaching your first-class pleasure, and attaining your full potential.

Thinking vs. Feeling Your Way Through Life

Focus for a moment on why being an intellectual is important to successful living.m

Suppose you take your car to a mechanic, and he tells you that you need a new fuel injector, which will cost $600. When you ask the mechanic how he knows you need a new fuel injector, he says:

"Simple. I put my hands on the hood of the car while the engine's running, and I 'feel' that the car needs a new fuel injector."

While this response might not seem so odd in parts of Berkeley or Sedona, in the real world would it be compelling enough for you to spend $600? How about $50? For most people, it's not. The mechanic's feelings about your car have no relation whatsoever to the reality of the situation. You need facts, not feelings, in order to make a decision.

When you are dealing with something as relatively insignificant as a few hundred dollars, you recognize that it is *understanding,* not feelings, that gives you an accurate picture of reality. Ironically, however, when it comes to some of the bigger issues in life, people often choose to live by what their emotions tell them, rather than by what their minds tell them.

In the Spring of 2000, Fox television broadcast a show entitled "Who Wants to Marry a Multimillionaire." The show was a contest among 50 women, competing to marry a man whom they had never met. All they knew was that he was a multimillionaire. The winner of this contest was a surgical nurse. As things turned out, the man was only a borderline millionaire with a restraining order filed by an ex-girlfriend. The show had tremendous fallout. The winner lost her nursing job because of negative publicity, and her life was transformed. Afterward, in an interview with *People Magazine,* she stated that appearing on the show was one of the worst decisions of her life.

So why had she originally decided to go on the show? As she explained, not much thought went into the decision. She needed a break after a stressful period in her life, and had a romantic notion about who this mystery millionaire could be. Not once did she truly consider the implications of her decision. She considered neither what the show represented—that woman are primarily interested in marrying for money and men are only interested in physical attraction—nor what would happen if she in fact won the contest. She acted in disregard of the depth of the decision that she was making, one that involved joining her life with that of a made-for-TV stranger.

The show's impact demonstrates the superficial way in which we often approach issues of tremendous consequence. We often make life-altering decisions without any deep analysis:

> with financial investments...
> *"I had a feeling that the stock would go up."*

> with major purchases...
> *"I saw it and I just had to have it."*

> with elections...
> *"I voted for him, because he seemed so sincere."*

Making Informed Decisions

The dating and marriage scene is rife with ill-conceived decision-making. When asked which is more important, finding a job or finding a spouse, most people say "finding a spouse." Yet they are often generally far less serious about looking for a mate. When looking for a job, people do research, get career counseling, and go to headhunters. People have a very clear idea of the type of job they seek, and can spend a significant amount of energy and time pursuing it.

On the other hand, how do some people look for a mate? They go to bars, clubs and parties awash in alcohol. How seriously would you consider a job to be CEO of a multi-million dollar company if an inebriated Chairman of the Board offered you the position through glazed eyes at a noisy bash? Yet people accept all types of alcohol-besotted offers for much more serious relationships. Is it any wonder then that many of them are surprised when life didn't turn out exactly as anticipated?

Even though most of us admit that living according to how we "feel" can be foolhardy, we often make major decisions without thoroughly considering the implications. This is because feelings and desires can easily cloud our perception of reality. And it's what makes con men so successful.

We all want financial success, and if someone promises an easy road to riches we often jump at it. Scam artists have a knack for manipulating this human impulse. A true story that confirms how easily people can be manipulated is told by Larry Williams in his book, *The Definitive Guide To Futures Trading:*[1]

> A trader sent letters to 10,000 potential clients advising a particular trade, to half he told buy and to half he told sell. To the half that profited from the advice, he sent another set of letters, again telling half to buy and half to sell. Then once again, to the group which profited, he sent one more set of letters. At the end of this process, he had 1,250 potential clients, who saw him making three correct predictions with uncanny foresight. To these, he offered a subscription to his investor newsletter for $500— a small price to pay for a source to the perfect trade. Obviously, many were duped by this offer.

This example shows that when we allow our emotions to guide our actions without rational investigation, we are focusing on the result we want and not on the reality of the underlying situation. This can be very dangerous.

Intellect Guides the Emotions

Becoming an intellectual does not just mean using your brain to solve problems. It is an approach to life where your intellect guides your emotions. This has a profound practical significance. How many times have you lost your temper with a store clerk or a help desk representative, when all they're doing is following a set of rules beyond their control? Even if it is emotionally satisfying, what good does it do to berate these individuals? Does it get you to your desired end?

Consider the following story related by Dale Carnegie[2] about one of history's greatest intellectuals, Abraham Lincoln:

> President Lincoln was plagued by a series of incredibly inept generals at the head of the Army of the Potomac, who one after

---

[1] Williams, Larry R. *The Definitive Guide to Futures Trading.* Windsor Books (Brightwaters, NY, 1989). Chapter 6—"On The Dark Side," pp. 93-118.

[2] Carnegie, Dale. *How to Win Friends and Influence People.* Pocket Books (New York, 1998). pp. 9-11.

the other never failed to miss a tremendous opportunity to defeat the enemy and bring a swift end to the war. After the Battle of Gettysburg, the Confederate Army under General Lee retreated to the banks of the Potomac and was trapped. It would have been easy prey for a continued assault by the North. Lincoln wired General Mead and ordered an immediate attack. Instead, the general called a council of war, which provided Lee with the time he needed to escape across the river. Beset by yet another obvious failure, Lincoln wrote a scathing letter to Mead. However, being an intellectual, Lincoln realized that sending such a letter would serve no constructive purpose. It would neither assist his cause of getting his general staff to comply with his demands, nor would it rectify the lost opportunity. So he placed the letter in his desk never to be sent.

Lincoln was a leader, a mover of men, and he understood when and how to push people to get a desired result.

When we are confronted with momentary frustrations, it is easy to give in to anger. But once we do, we stop being rational. It takes two to fight. When you have the presence of mind *not* to take the bait of a provocative act or comment, you are using your mind to control your adrenaline and resist a fruitless confrontation.

The intellectual trains the self to be in control with a two-step process:

✳ Realizing that it is within your power to have such control

✳ Developing a willingness to step back from any situation so you can access this control.

Instead of just reacting to events, you need to stop, review the facts, and have your intellect take charge.

> A real intellectual is profoundly practical. Because you think, you are the person most likely to act; and because you think before acting, the action is likely to be reasonable, practical and effective.

This doesn't mean you should ignore your feelings. It simply means that when making important decisions, it's critical to distinguish your intellectual from your emotional response. If you use your intellect to direct your life, rather than your feelings, you have a much better chance of accomplishing your goals.

Michael Polanyi, author of the book *Personal Knowledge: Towards A Post-Critical Philosophy*, provides a link between reason and feeling in his discussion of "intellectual passions."[3] A personal and deeply felt passion for discovery is what drives a scientist to explore, to accumulate evidence, to test and research until the facts are perceived. An intellectual passion means *caring so much about something that you are willing to take the time and effort to fully consider your actions before acting.*

If you care passionately about your country, you decide to vote based on extensive and careful research into the candidates' platforms and voting histories. Such an important decision cannot be based on a candidate's wit, charm or winning smile. When you care passionately, you base major decisions on the study of relevant factors, such as buying a new car on relevant factors like gas mileage, safety records and comfort features.

In his book, *Emotional Intelligence*,[4] Daniel Goleman highlights the important role of emotions in effective decision-making. He demonstrates that emotional intelligence—the ability to motivate yourself, to persist under adverse circumstances, to control impulses, to regulate moods—is a better indicator of your potential for success than IQ.

> A person of great emotional intelligence is not a person devoid of emotion, but a person in touch with and in control of his emotions. In a word, such a person is an intellectual.

---

[3] Polanyi, Michael. *Personal Knowledge: Towards A Post-Critical Philosophy.* University of Chicago Press (Chicago 1962). "Intellectual Passions," pp. 171-174.

[4] Goleman, Daniel. *Emotional Intelligence.* Bantam Books (New York, 1995). Chapter 3—"When Smart is Dumb," pp. 33-36

Success at living requires that we use our minds, rather than our emotions, to control the bottom line. This is the essence of intellectualism. However, the intellectual does not attain this status overnight. Someone does not begin a career as lead musician for the New York Philharmonic by waking up one morning, having never played a note, and thinking "why don't I give this instrument a shot," although this may very well work for a hip-hop group. Intellectual behavior requires training.

To master your intellectual abilities you must pass through a series of skill levels, just as martial arts experts progress through a series of "belts." You can apply a similar process to intellectual training. Each successive belt identifies greater skill at using your mind for living. The eventual goal is to train yourself to become a black belt intellectual.

Exercises~

❶ Name several people that you believe are intellectuals. Why do you believe that they should be characterized as such? Would you say that these people were more emotional thinkers or more rational thinkers?

❷ Do you believe that by nature some people are more rational thinkers and some people more emotional thinkers? Do you agree that achieving goals is more effectively achieved through rational thought as opposed to emotional thought? How would you describe the connection between rational and emotional thinking.

❸ In London, Siamese twins were born connected at the chest. They shared certain vital organs, such as the heart, which resided primarily in the body of one of the children. If the children were surgically separated, the one in whom these organs resided had an excellent chance of surviving and living a normal life. However, the operation would surely kill the other child. If nothing were to be done, both would surely die in a matter of weeks or months, because of the strain on the shared organs. The parents for religious reasons decided against an operation. Their rationale was that life is in God's hands, and they are prohibited from taking any action, which will actively cause the death of another. The hospital petitioned the court for instructions. Imagine that you are the judge! How do you decide and why?

The White Belt Intellectual: Know What You Are Talking About

An intellectual is a clear thinker, always striving to attain greater *clarity* about the key issues in life. The first step in the process of becoming an intellectual is to learn to define terms—*to know what you are talking about*. Without precise definitions, you can't understand any subject for yourself, or express your ideas about it to someone else.

If someone asked "Are you a student?" you'd find it easy to answer. You know what a student is—someone who attends a school—and you know whether you currently meet the necessary criteria.

But if that person asked "are you a catechumen," you might respond "Well, I don't know. What's that?" If the questioner persisted in spite of your response, saying "Don't ask me that, just tell me, are you or aren't you," you would have to say, "I can't tell you, because I don't know what you're talking about." *Without a definition you simply cannot answer the question.*

Now suppose someone asked whether you are a good person. The overwhelming majority of people respond to this query affirmatively. Is your answer a resounding *"yes"* as well?

But wait—do you really know what a good person is? Many people who answer the question don't have a clear definition of what it means to be a good person. They simply don't know what they are talking about.

Since most people have not really thought through the question of what it means to be a good person, they base their response on their feelings. They answer the question affirmatively because they feel it's better to be good. When pressed to define the nature of a good person, people often use negatives; a good person does not steal, cheat, or murder. Then again, neither does a corpse.

The problem is that we still do not know what a good person *is*, and we all desire to be one.

Since a central objective in our lives is to be good, wouldn't it make sense to figure out whether we are reaching that goal? *Plenty of people have sacrificed their lives for causes they "felt" were good when in reality those causes were evil. How many terrorists have died for what they mistakenly felt was a just cause? In reality, they died as evil men, without ever having accomplished their goal of being good.* Clearly, we need a way of measuring our success.

If you use your mind rather than your feelings to direct your life, you'll have a much better chance of accurately perceiving reality and of accomplishing your goals. The first step in this process is *defining your terms*. Always think about whether you know what you are talking about. We need definitions for all issues in life: What is a good person? What is love? What is friendship? What is stubborn? What is intolerant? What is a "processing fee" on a mortgage closing statement? Once you have good definitions, they become your cornerstones for a rational, successful way of life.

Aiming at the Target

A person who does not have definitions is like the child in the following fable:

> A king was walking through the forest and noticed that many of the trees were painted with bull's eyes. Unfailingly, within each bull's eye, there was an arrow. And some of the targets were painted in extremely challenging positions. The king was so

impressed with this display of archery that he sent out a search party to find the archer. Up ahead, they discovered a 10-year-old boy. The king asked incredulously, "Are you responsible for these bull's eyes?" "Yes," the boy replied.

The king then requested that the boy train all of his soldiers to shoot with such accuracy. "It's really no big deal," the boy said. "Anyone can do it. I'll show you." The boy took out an arrow, fired it into a tree, and then picked up a paintbrush and painted a target around the arrow.

Living without definitions is like first shooting an arrow and then painting the target around it. We feel our actions are on target, only to find ourselves chasing the arrow afterward.

Exercises~

❶ While the most important application of definitions is in the conduct of your own life, awareness of the importance of proper definitions can make you a more critical and intelligent consumer of goods and of political ideas. Read the two following speech extracts, both made by famous public figures. (The speakers are identified on the page 100.) Which words would you ask the speaker to define, if you were in attendance at this speech? In which cases *does* the speaker define important terms?

Excerpt One~

To me the situation of [our nation] today seems like that of a sick person. I know that people on various sides often say, "Why do you constantly say that we are sick?" People have said to us: "Daily life goes on as it always did; this 'sick person,' as you can see, eats day after day, works day in and day out; how can you say that this person is sick?" But the question is not whether a nation is still alive and the economy functioning. Just because a person eats and works does not mean that he is fit. The most reliable criterion is how that person himself feels. He can tell whether he is fit or ill. It is precisely the same in the life of nations. Nations are often sick for long periods—often centuries—yet individual members of the nations cannot fully understand the nature of the sickness.

Excerpt Two~

You are not all going to die. Only two percent of you right here today would die in a major battle. Death must not be feared. Death, in time, comes to all men. Yes, every man is scared in his first battle. If he says he's not, he's a liar. Some men are cowards but they fight the same as the brave men or they get the hell slammed out of them watching men fight who are just as scared as they are. The real hero is the man who fights even though he is scared. Some men get over their fright in a minute under fire. For some, it takes an hour. For some, it takes days. But a real man will never let his fear of death overpower his honor, his sense of duty to his country, and his innate manhood.

❷ Look for other examples of public speeches and/or advertisements in which important terms are or are not clearly defined.

❸ Is it intolerant to believe you are right and everyone else is wrong and to try and convince them of the same? If not, how would you define intolerance?

❹ Name five traits that you would like to be known for. Now define those terms.

The Orange Belt Intellectual:
Use Your Definitions—Say What You Mean

The first step to becoming an intellectual is defining important terms. The next step is employing those terms. An orange belt not only *seeks* definitions, but also *uses* them. As an Orange Belt Intellectual, *you say exactly what you mean.*

This is a real problem for most people:

They say this	But they really mean this
"Will do."	I'll try…
"I can't."	I don't want to…
"I know."	I think so…
"Trust me."	Gotcha…

We all have to use our words judiciously. Otherwise we confuse issues.

> By not saying what we truly mean, we create problems where we later have to justify our actions because the people who heard us expected different outcomes.

When an employee says she can finish a report by a particular date, her employer expects her to have the job completed on time. When a husband tells his wife he'll be home at 6:00 p.m., she expects him to arrive at that time. When promises are made, it doesn't matter if the report is delayed because the statistics department failed to provide necessary data, or if the husband is late because an important client called at 5:45. You lose relationship capital when your assur-

---

Excerpt One in box on page 99 is from a speech given by Adolph Hitler on Jan. 18, 1927, to an audience composed of a broad spectrum of Germans, at a rally organized by the National Socialist Party.

Excerpt Two from the box on page 99 is from a speech given by General George Patton on June 5, 1944, to Allied troops, somewhere in England.

ances can't be trusted. In the end, people are ultimately judged by their actual performance.

And people are far too casual about the way they speak and the words they choose. A survey cited in the book, *The Day America Told the Truth*,[5] reports that 91% of Americans lie on a regular basis. Clearly, the average person's word bears little true meaning.

How would you respond to the question, "Are you happy?" Again, most people answer "yes" without giving the question serious thought. They are not miserable and they desire happiness, so they answer the question positively. But such affirmative answers contain little significance. Unless people have a clear definition in their minds for the term "happy," their response is likely to be inaccurate. When asked to explain the meaning of their words, people just fit their current mood into the concept of happiness.

> **Happiness is the emotional state that results from taking pleasure in what you currently have. It is not agitating over what you don't yet have but want to acquire, or brooding over mistakes in your past and what could have been.**

The only way to know if you really are happy is to use such a definition to analyze your current situation. Can you derive satisfaction from your good health, family situation, financial resources, and other circumstances of good fortune?

You might realize that you are not really happy because of a disproportionate focus on unfulfilled desires. Without applying this definition, you will never know if you are aiming your life on target. You may also never know that there is a level of joy out there, which far exceeds your present state.

---

[5] Patterson, James & Peter, Kim. *The Day America Told the Truth: What People Really Believe About Everything That Really Matters.* Prentice Hall Press (New York, 1991). pp. 45-51.

The "I-You-He" Paradigm

The *I-You-He Paradigm* demonstrates how people are driven by subjectivity. It shows us how human beings tend to color reality based on their feelings, and how applying definitions helps people attain greater clarity.

The I-You-He Paradigm works as follows:

❋ When we are referring to ourselves, we always paint a picture in the best, whitest possible light.

❋ When we disagree with someone, we do not want to insult this person face to face, so we paint a gray picture.

❋ When we are talking about someone who is not around, we are safe to paint the situation black.

So "I" is white, "You" is gray, and "He" is black. In life, this is how the I-You-He Paradigm might be expressed:

> You are a passenger in a car careening at 90 mph down a winding road. As you grip the dashboard in terror, you turn to the driver and say, "Aren't you being foolhardy?" In defense, the driver responds, "Me? I'm not afraid of a few turns. I'm brave." Once you get out of the car, you are likely to tell a friend, "That guy's a reckless idiot!"

The driver refers to himself as "brave." To his face, you tell him that he is "foolhardy." Behind his back, you express your true emotions, "he's a reckless idiot." Which reality is correct? Only by working through objective definitions can we accurately assess the situation:

❋ *Brave* means taking necessary risks for a worthwhile purpose (e.g. rushing into a burning building to save a child trapped inside).

❋ *Foolhardy* means taking unnecessary risks, yet for a noble cause (e.g. rushing into the burning building without protective gear).

✳ *Reckless* means taking unnecessary risks for no worthwhile cause (e.g. rushing into the burning building to watch the beams on fire).

Now with these definitions, even the driver has to admit that he was being reckless. Speeding 90 miles an hour on a winding mountain road, he was taking unnecessary risks with his own life and the lives of others for no good purpose.

When you have clear definitions and apply them, you escape the trap of subjectivity. You then have the tools necessary to assess your actions as well as the actions of others.

This is the Orange Belt Intellectual. The Orange Belt considers definitions and the meaning of words before speaking. Orange Belt Intellectuals measure what they say according to their definitions, and the definitions show how on-target they really are.

Exercises~

❶ Reconsider the five traits that you would like to be known for, as outlined in the previous exercises. What types of behavior will you need to engage in so that your reputation will become associated with these characteristics?

❷ A friend buys a painting, and with great pride invites you to come view it. You know the painting was quite expensive, but you think that it is hideous. When your friend asks for your opinion, do you lie, tell the truth, or change the subject?

❸ A friend is abusing drugs. The friend seems to be having difficulties in many areas of his life, but the friend assures you that he is in control of his habit. You have your doubts. What do you do?

The Red Belt Intellectual: Mean What You Say— Connect Your Emotion to Your Intellect

As a White Belt Intellectual you begin to define terms, and as an Orange Belt you scrupulously attempt to use them—to say what you mean. The distinguishing mark of the Red Belt Intellectual is to *mean what you say*.

When you mean what you say, you maintain a consistency between your inner self and your outer self. As a Red Belt Intellectual, you don't say one thing with your lips, while truly believing something else in your heart. A Red Belt Intellectual has *integrity*.

Integrity requires that when you realize that something is true and accept it intellectually, you need to act on that basis. People of integrity take what they understand and make it a part of themselves. As a Red Belt Intellectual, your emotions are guided and controlled by the intellect.

When you really believe something, you need to be consistent about it in your beliefs, speech and actions. The problem is that while people may understand something is true, they don't make an effort to connect their ideas to their emotions. People whose convictions are disconnected from their feelings are anti-intellectual.

You see an obvious examples of anti-intellectual behavior everyday. On every advertisement or billboard hawking cigarettes, and on the outside of every cigarette package itself is the warning, "The Surgeon General has determined that cigarette smoking is hazardous to your health." Could it be that smokers are unaware of the risk of lung cancer and heart disease caused by smoking? Of course not.

With this reality, why are there millions of smokers? Most smokers will admit that smoking is dangerous. If you asked them, "would you ever do something that you knew was dangerous to your health and could kill you?" they would say "no." Yet, they will still continue to smoke. The desire to smoke obscures the reality. People who smoke have not integrated their knowledge of the dangers of smoking into their being; their intellectual understanding has not permeated their feelings. They rationalize away the danger. Their emotional desire prevents them from truly believing that smoking is dangerous.

For these unfortunate smokers, the practical knowledge succumbs to their feelings. The same is true with all bad habits. The anti-intellectual fails to translate his understanding of good behavior into feelings and then action. Sometimes it takes a major dose of reality—such as a heart attack—to force feelings into line with understanding.

To be a Red Belt Intellectual, thoughts and ideas must influence the way you act. You must put rational understanding into your feelings. A bad habit like smoking has to become something you do not "feel" like doing.

Exercises~

❶ You have been assigned to present an anti-drug presentation to sixth-graders. What arguments would you use to convince them not to use drugs? Do you think these arguments will be effective? Why or why not?

❷ Watch the documentary film *Scared Straight* or *Final Exit: Extreme Reality*. What is the objective of these films? Do you think that they are an effective means of achieving their goals?

❸ List five actions that you can take tomorrow that will further associate your reputation with the five traits that you identified in the exercises at the end of the prior two lessons. What attitudes do you need to have in order to facilitate acting in these ways?

The Brown Belt Intellectual: Live With What You Mean

You'll know you're a Brown Belt Intellectual when you not only say what you mean and mean what you say, but also *live with what you mean*. Living with what you mean is taking control of your life so that it becomes a positive expression of the ideals you hold to be true.

As a Brown Belt, you will clarify what you want to say and do *before* speaking and acting in order to be sure that all of your actions are in line with your values. Within this category, there are three "degrees," or ways your mind works proactively to guide you through life.

The First-Degree Brown Belt

A first-degree Brown Belt seeks a moment-by-moment consciousness of his or her behavior in order to *act* upon life's challenges, as opposed to *reacting* to them. As a brown belt, you need to constantly ask yourself, "What am I doing and why?"

If, for example, someone in your home has the habit of returning late at night in a very loud manner, instead of simply reacting to this behavior, you need to ask yourself, "What do I want to accomplish?" A Brown Belt Intellectual knows that yelling is generally ineffective—particularly over the long run—and instead focuses on the goal: "My goal is to get my roommate to shut the door behind her when she enters the room late at night."

Only with such a goal clearly in mind can you set a proper course of action. A fitting response might be installing soft padding on the doorframe, or placing a reminder note on the door, or finding something that your roommate wants that you can give in exchange more considerate behavior.

Acting and not reacting is not only a matter of how you address overt negative stimuli; it is applicable to more subtle situations as well. The question of "what am I trying to accomplish" is applicable throughout the day. When you come home in the evening, you need to consider your goal. Is it to escape the pressures of your classroom or office or is it to do something positive to facilitate self-growth? You may have the choice of turning on the TV or spending time with the family.

Exercises~

❶ Consider the last argument that you had. Describe the events leading up to it. What do you think you could have done to have avoided the confrontation? Was there an alternative that could have yielded better results?

❷ Spend ten minutes each evening for the next week keeping a journal. Record your major plans and goals for the next day, and evaluate how well you succeeded in accomplishing your goals of the previous day. After a week, consider whether this was a worthwhile exercise.

❸ In one to two pages write an essay, which encapsulates your personal philosophy of life. Make a list of five major goals that you would like to accomplish in your lifetime. Choose one goal and devise a plan to achieve it.

The Second-Degree Brown Belt

The second-degree Brown Belt plans the entire day. Every night before going to bed, the Brown Belt considers *what, how and why* he is going to do tomorrow. Then at the end of the following day, he evaluates the outcome to see whether he met his goals. The second-degree Brown Belt tries to understand why some plans succeeded and others failed, and makes adjustments to improve future results.

Are you going to read the newspaper tomorrow morning? Why? Know your goal. If it is to become informed, then decide beforehand how much time you should spend on this. Do you want to have a more loving relationship with a family member? How will you go about it? What about your relaxation time in the evening? Is there a better way to spend it? Think about your whole day and plan it out for maximum advantage.

The second-degree Brown Belt lives each day the way a serious businessperson plans his or her schedule. Just as an executive slots important events in advance, the Brown Belt intellectual carefully plans each day. Successful businesspeople do not just come to work, waiting to see what will come through the door. Instead, they're in control.

As a second-degree Brown Belt, you know what you are going to do in advance, why you are going to do it, and how. Do you want to wake up in the morning on the wrong side of the bed, groaning, or do you want to wake up fresh and invigorated?

The Third-Degree Brown Belt

As a third-degree Brown Belt, you focus on the big picture: planning your life.

You need to ask yourself "What am I living for? What is the purpose of existence? What do I want to accomplish with my life?" As a third-degree Brown Belt you use your mind to constantly refine and aim your life in a direction that will accomplish your deepest goals.

Exercises~

❶ Consider the last argument that you had. What were the events leading up to it? What do you think you could have done to have avoided the confrontation? Was there an alternative that could have yielded better results?

❷ Spend ten minutes each evening for the next week keeping a journal. Record your major plans and goals for the next day, and evaluate how well you succeeded in accomplishing your goals of the previous day. After a week, consider whether this was a worthwhile exercise.

❸ Write a one- to two-page essay that encapsulates your personal philosophy of life. Make a list of five major goals that you would like to accomplish in your lifetime. Choose one goal and devise a plan to achieve it.

The Black Belt Intellectual: Make Every Action Reflect Your Goals

So far you've learned how to think clearly and honestly, defining your terms and consistently applying these definitions. You have learned that you need to control your emotions so that your mind directs your heart. You have learned how to plan your actions in order to express your internalized emotions. And, you are ready to live your life in accordance with your principles.

The final step is to live your ideal life 24 hours a day.

Black Belt Intellectuals are constantly aware of the connection between their actions and their life plan. They are always asking "does this bring me closer or push me further away from where I want to go, and how do my choices reflect my ultimate desires?"

As a third degree Brown Belt Intellectual you solidified the three connections between thought and feeling that you developed as a Red Belt Intellectual.

* You first work to master the immediate situation. One who reacts is controlled by one's emotional response; one who acts thoughtfully takes advantage of the available options.

✳ Next, you plan your short-term goals, scheduling the events of your day.

✳ Finally, you look to see how your life fits into the greater scheme of things. You constantly consider and reassess your long-range goals so that you don't merely drift along on the tide of life. You consider the person you want to become and the principles you live by.

> When you reach this level, every moment of every day is part of the plan to take you where you want to go, give you what you want to achieve, and turn you into who you want to become.

As a Black Belt, you take this process a step further—*to live a thoroughly integrated existence.* As a Black Belt, your moment-by-moment actions reflect your long-term goals, which in turn mirror the type of person you are. Principles and values are not just theoretical ideas—they are key elements in the way Black Belts conduct their lives. Thoughts are not devoid of emotion, and emotions are not unbridled by the lack of thought.

The Black Belt is neither a radical running headlong into a cause, nor an apathetic bystander in the world. Instead, the Black Belt is emotionally charged and excited about life, and spurred forward to follow her dreams and aspirations. More than nine to five, the Black Belt lives five to nine as well. The Black Belt Intellectual wakes up in the morning saying, "It's great to be alive."

As a Black Belt, you plan your life and live it. Indeed, the Black Belt says, "Life is everything I want and more."

Giving To Take vs. Giving To Give

Consider the scenario we examined previously of the housemate who didn't know how to shut the door gently at night. The Black Belt would not simply be trying to train the housemate's behavior as it connected to that moment. Instead, the Black Belt would see the overall connection of how this challenge relates to her role as a human being: The Black Belt thinks "How do I want to behave towards others and how do I want others to perceive and relate to me?"

When the Black Belt sits down at the end of the day to review and plan the next 24 hours, it is not a routine action taken in isolation from long-term desires. It is a part of an ongoing personal refinement. When the Black Belt considers long-term goals and life plan, she is not mired in a narcissistic process of self-involvement. Instead, she is developing self-awareness and gaining a sense of her place in the world. This lets the Black Belt be truly giving, and fully relate to her external environment.

Precisely because the Black Belt Intellectual knows who she is and her place in the world, she senses a deep connection to the outside world. Her giving is a form of self-expression.

In life, there are two types of people: *Those who give to take, and those who give to give.* Non-intellectuals, who go through life led by their emotions, are likely throw themselves into cause after cause. However, this is not true giving, because they have no self to give. Instead, non-intellectuals give to others to fill their own selves up. They extract self-worth from the external world because they cannot produce it themselves. They have no real identity of their own so they take in life and meaning from outside. Their giving is actually taking.

Black Belt Intellectuals have something to give—themselves. In giving, they actually transfer part of themselves to the larger world. The Black Belt Intellectual becomes the person most able to connect intimately with the entire world around him. Such vision empowers a person to expand well beyond himself.

Rising Through the Ranks

The first intellectual level is to formulate definitions. The second is to use these definitions to evaluate how you feel and think about any given subject. The third is to fully understand a subject so it influences how you feel about it, rather than letting your feelings control your thoughts. The fourth is to have your mind guide and plan your life. The final level is to do all of this on a constant basis and live in accordance with your long term goals. This lets you become the ultimate giving and relating individual—and helps you get your fair share of the pleasure you deserve.

Exercises~

❶ In one page describe the person you want to become. What things would you want people to eulogize you for?

❷ Write a one-page description of your perfect day today. Now write a one-page description of what your perfect day will be fifteen years from now. If they're different, what will you do with your day tomorrow to start getting to that future point?

❸ You are a young idealistic lawyer. You want to become the best trial lawyer possible so that you can eventually pick your own clients and defend just causes. To get the experience necessary, the best avenues open to you are either joining the public defender's office (in which case you will at times be forced to defend despicable human beings) or joining the district attorney's office (in which case you will at times be forced to prosecute people that you personally feel may be innocent). In either case, you cannot choose your clients and will likely have to act contrary to your personal belief system. Nevertheless, these avenues will best ensure that you are able to achieve your ultimate life goals. What do you do?

chapter 5

Putting *it* All Together

This book began with the observation that, for the most part, people formulate their values and act based on knowledge conveyed to them by their societies. Well, we've come a long way since then, and this is the chapter where you will put it all together to achieve the highest level of pleasure.

So, before we continue on to the ultimate reward, let's take a few seconds to review all you have learned so far:

* You learned that informed decision-making requires the ability to step out of your circumstances to reach a level of objectivity in order to judge the morality of your own behavior.

* Next, you saw that people are motivated by pleasure and that various, qualitatively distinct, levels of pleasure exist in the world. Your challenge is to choose a course in life that will lead them to the greatest amount of pleasure.

* In analyzing what constitutes effective choice, you learned that making good choices is a function of your free will. Moreover, by actualizing your freewill, you alter the point at which your choices are a function of your free will. Personal development comes from directing this growth process.

* You learned that "intellectualism" is not some kind of affected form of showing off your intelligence. Rather, it empowers you to direct your self-growth. As an intellectual, you simply strive for clarity in understanding the world and in finding your place in it. Becoming an intellectual is about figuring out who you are, who you want to become, and regularly conducting a personal accounting. This exercise

113

also leads to a deepening of your connection to your social and physical environments, and brings you to a place of being thoroughly consistent in thought and action, to being a person of integrity.

✳ Intellectualism is an expression of the power of free will in a specific aspect of the human condition. Free will views the battle of life in terms of the struggle between growth and entropy, and intellectualism focuses on how this struggle is manifest in the mind as the tension between objective and subjective reasoning. Therefore, the elements of free will and intellectualism mirror each other.

✳ As an intellectual, your quest for clarity through definitions is the free will actor's striving for awareness.

✳ The application of these definitions, which allows you to escape the necessity of having to justify words and behavior after-the-fact and enables you to assume responsibility from the outset, and is indeed a component of independence.

✳ Finally, unifying of all of your actions to reflect your life goals is directing the growth process. In the end, the trait of integrity which results as a byproduct of this "intellectualism" is an expression of the great potential of free will to take full control of your life, and indeed your entire reality, through informed and reasoned decision-making.

Back To the "A" of Life

This understanding of the dynamics of decision-making returns us now to the topic of analysis with which we began this course, namely the "A" of life. Assuming that the processes we have outlined can indeed make you into a more effective decision-maker, our discussion still needs to address how you can be sure that your value choices are based on truth and not determined by forces outside yourself.

You also need to know how you can be sure that what you think reflects an objective understanding and is not really skewed by your subjective wants and desires. If you cannot attain this clarity to know that you are in control of your decisions, and that your decisions are rooted in reality, then you can never be sure that you are pursuing real pleasure or that your moral and ethical growth is not a fallacious illusion.

To resolve this dilemma, you need to address the *essential* issue of what is knowledge:

* How can you be sure of anything?

* How do you know what you know?

* How do you know that what you perceive corresponds to reality?

* How do you know who you are?

* In today's complex and multi-faceted world, is it possible to achieve certainty of anything?

At first glance, these questions seem a bit trite. Yet, these same questions have boggled the minds of philosophers throughout history. And the answers, as you shall see, do impact on your life.

Achieving Five-Finger Clarity

To begin formulating answers, begin by examining a simple issue, such as the fact that all people are confident that they have five fingers on each hand (unless, of course, a person is a polydactyl, in which case he or she would be confident of a different number).

There is a popular notion that you need to hear all points of view before coming to a conclusion. But, have you ever heard a point of view that people have 7 fingers or 20 fingers or 90 fingers? If you did hear such a view, would it be necessary to investigate? Of course not! Everyone knows that people have five fingers on each hand, barring an accident or birth defect. You can look and count. A popular philosophical notion also exists that absolute truth does not exist. But, is anybody not absolutely certain that people have absolutely five fingers on each hand?

Human beings are susceptible to influence under pressure. Brainwashing, or coercive persuasion, is a real phenomenon. People can be manipulated to change their thoughts and beliefs. Cults exist and have a success rate. Studies show that ex-cult members often suffer from Post-traumatic Stress Disorder. Groups such as the Branch Davidians and the Jim Jones' People's Temple were filled with followers who had been normal, upstanding, community members but were convinced to sell everything and eventually even give up their lives. China under Mao during the Cultural Revolution effectively employed similar processes. From the Korean and Vietnam Wars, there are stories of patriotic soldiers, who after indoctrination were ready to vilify Western imperialism. These events show that people often do not have complete confidence in their beliefs and can be manipulated.

Knowing these facts, would you be willing to take the risk of exposing yourself to the indoctrination of a cult?[1] How about your children?

Many people would not be willing to walk into the Moonies or Hare Krishna organizations, or anyone of a number of other groups, and say, "Here I am. I'm ready to spend a month with you folks. I'm so confident of what I believe and that you guys are wrong, that I have no qualms about hearing you out." Given their success rate in creating "true believers," you might be justified in being a little afraid that you may just come out believing that Reverend Moon is God or some other central tenet of their belief system.

Nevertheless, despite the obvious fact that people can be influenced, even cult followers could never be brainwashed into believing that they have 75 fingers, no matter how intense, skillful or painful the indoctrination. People might lose confidence in the policies of their country or convinced to take up a new ideology, but what people know, they know. There are limits to brainwashing, and these limits are restricted to the areas in which doubt exists. When we do not have "five-finger" clarity about what we believe, then we are subject to influence.

---

[1] If you are very confident in answering this question in the affirmative, then read carefully some of *Suggested Readings* for Chapter 5.

In order to gain that confidence, we need to delve further into the question of how it is that we come to "know" things, and on what basis we know them.

> The issue is whether and how can you attain this same degree of confidence—this five-finger clarity—in your world outlook, in your philosophy of life, and in the values you live by.

Know Who You Are

Do you know who you are?

As a starting point in your quest to understand how it is that you know anything, conduct the following experiment. Take it seriously, and it will focus your attention on how perplexing it can be to "know what you know," and how susceptible human beings are to suggestion when they lack clarity:

Concentrate for a moment and try to imagine that your name is John (or Jane) Axelrod. You are a lawyer from El Paso, Texas. You are now a tourist walking down a street in London, England, and you see a sign that says "John Axelrod—El Paso—London—Lawyer."

You think to yourself, "What a coincidence! I've got to meet this guy."

You knock on the door, and a man answers saying, "Come on in. Who are you?"

You respond, "Well, I'm John Axelrod."

"John Axelrod! Isn't that a coincidence! Where are you from? What do you do?"

You say, "I'm from El Paso, and I'm a lawyer."

"That's amazing," says the man from London. "Tell me, where do you live?"

"10 Clark Lane."

"10 Clark Lane! What are you talking about, that's my El Paso address!" The fellow from London frowns at you and continues, "What's your father's name?"

"Steven."

"What's your mother's name?"

"Alice."

"Well that's my father and my mother. Hey, you're a fraud! You're assuming my identity!"

The man from London is accusing *you* of assuming *his* identity.

Try to imagine, how you would begin to feel just about now? What emotions would you be feeling—confusion, anger? You know that in abnormal psychology sometimes a person will assume another's identity. The more ambitious people focus on great figures like Napoleon, but maybe, some people look at Napoleon and say, "Nah, I don't want to rule the world. That's too complicated. A nice looking guy like a John Axelrod would be so much easier. So, I want to be him." Perhaps you are thinking, "Maybe he is criminal who has stolen my identity."

The man from London calls the police. They are coming down to his office. Who do you think they are going to arrest? This man has a reputation in London. He is John Axelrod, the lawyer from El Paso. He has his business and his clients. He is a known quantity. You, on the other hand, are from out of town.

With the police are orderlies in white coats from the local mental hospital, and you have got to convince them who you are. So, you reach for your passport. It will contain the evidence you need: Your name—John Axelrod, with your picture and address. But—uh, oh—you lost your passport, or maybe it was stolen! What dreadful timing! What a shame that you lost it just now.

The man from London reaches into his pocket, and he has his passport! It says John Axelrod, with his picture and your address.

Whom are they going to take? Are you crazy? Are you still sure that you are you? Would you still feel that you are John Axelrod from El Paso? If so, how do you know you are right? How do you know who you are? And, how do you prove it?

Do you see that some people with less of a grip on how they know something could really be disturbed at this point? Maybe the other guy is right. Maybe you were brainwashed, and you only think you are John Axelrod from El Paso. Maybe you are someone else. Maybe you got into an accident, and the doctors did this to you. Maybe you are the victim of a terrible plot.

A proper London police officer approaches and says, "Well, can you prove that you're really John Axelrod?" Think fast! What do you say? Possibly, you say, "Let's call up Mom."

The man from London agrees. Now you'll prove it! You dial your mother. She gets on the phone. You say, "Mom!" She says, "Who's this?" You say, "Mom! It's me! This is no time to joke! I'm in trouble over here! Please, Mom...." She says, "What's going on? Who are you?" The other guy takes the phone, and she says, "Oh, John. Who was that character?"

What would you be thinking and feeling now? This has to be a plot! You do not understand what is going on, but now you know this guy is not a psychotic. This is a spy story! You are a victim, what do you do? Maybe you ought to be silent.

Are you still sure you're right—maybe you are crazy? You would have to have a pretty tight grip on reality under these circumstances to be sure of yourself. How can you prove that you are who you are?

You have to sit down with John Axelrod of London and some objective people and say, "Let's investigate: What address did you live at? How many rooms were in the house? Where is the kitchen? Are there stairs to the basement? How many steps? Who lives on the right? Who lives on the left? Who lives opposite you? Where's the nearest drugstore? What's the street on the corner?"

You have to seek out the facts; only then does reality become clear. John Axelrod may be able to fake you out to some extent, but no one can steal all the details of your life.

Know What You Know

To have clarity, to really know what you know—with five-finger certainty—you have to investigate and get the facts. You need to collect, in a dispassionate and systematic fashion, the *evidence* that will lead to accurate conclusions. This is the key to discovering truth amidst all the confusion. Five-finger certainty means that you *know*. You are not just harboring an assumption, an illusion, or a hallucination.

Knowing what you know gives you confidence in your beliefs.

Exercises~

❶ You have been framed for a murder that you did not commit. All the evidence is against you. There is no way to attack the physical evidence; it is airtight. What can you say in your defense?

❷ Watch the film *The Matrix*. How can you be sure that your reality is not like that in the movie; everything is just an illusion while our minds exist somewhere else? Does it matter?

❸ Watch the film *Twelve Angry Men*. If you were on a jury, and you were the lone voice to acquit a person of murder, do you think that you could withstand the pressure of the other voices against you?

Living by Default

Clarity of knowledge, knowing what you know, is exceedingly important, because people are subject to pressure. If everyone else in society held one view and you believed in an opposing point, you would have to be quite sure of yourself to maintain that belief, much less have the courage to act on it.

The application of this dynamic is not just a theoretical game about spies; rather, it is readily apparent in our daily lives. In the clothes we wear, the cars we drive, and the restaraunts we eat at, we live our lives following the latest trends. Social pressure and peer pressure are powerful forces influencing our lives.[2]

On a more fundamental level, as we discussed previously, learning to "know what you know" is essential, because the bulk of your convictions have been dictated to you by your society.

---

[2]See *Suggested Reading* number four under *Suggested Readings* for Chapter 5.

> Learning to understand on what basis you believe things is the only way to distinguish your true convictions from those maintained simply as a result of your socialization. Generally speaking these latter assumptions are the ones, which form the basis of most life-altering decisions.

We all appreciate that the society in which we grow up has a tremendous influence on the way we think. Natural citizens of America are most likely capitalists in their outlook. Had the same people been born in China, they would most probably be good Communists. A person born in Spain would undoubtedly be a Catholic, whereas a person born just a few miles south would be a Muslim. How earnestly these individuals believe in these ideologies is irrelevant; their belief in one and not the other is merely an accident of birth.

Every society produces people who are passionately convinced that their ideas and beliefs are right. Many are even willing to kill the other guy whom they believe is wrong, and to die themselves based on their commitment. What is really amazing is that by and large these people do not know how they know what they are doing is right; they do not know on what basis they are acting.

Consider the fact that the vast majority of human beings alive today are living on the basis of a very serious, very basic, error!

You might ask "How is this true?" The answer: Simple mathematics!

Consider that there are some two billion Christians in the world, one billion Moslems, three quarter of a billion Hindus and half a billion Buddhists (to name just the largest groups), and every one of them is saying that the others, the people who belong to the other religions, are wrong. Everybody is 100 percent sure they are right, and the other fellow by extension must necessarily be wrong. Only one thing is absolutely certain—they cannot all be right! Somebody may be right and the rest wrong, or everybody might be wrong. However, the absolute truth is that at least the overwhelming majority is mistaken.

If the Christians are right and Jesus died to atone for our sins, then the more than three billion people on earth who are not Christian are living in serious error. And there are grave consequences to the matter. On the other hand, if the Moslems are right, then more than four billion people on earth are wrong. In such a case, they ought to change their beliefs accordingly. It is simple mathematics!

Imagine Suni Iraqi setting off for a Shiite neighborhood in Baghdad to kill some people there. If someone were to catch his attention for a moment and ask, "Pardon me, but did you ever stop to consider that if you had been born just a couple of miles away, you would now be coming with your bomb to kill yourself?" He would be so sure that he was doing the right thing that he would not understand the question.

Suppose the Iraqi had been born in Serbia—he would also be convinced that he was right, but he would not be a Moslem, he would be a Christian on his way to kill Moslems. If he were born to a Catholic family in Northern Ireland, he might be a member of the IRA. If he were a young German in 1939, he might be a member of the National Socialist Party.

Relative Morality

Everyone's worldview is to a large extent predetermined by the mores and culture into which they are born. This being the case, since we demonstrated that the vast majority of people are living in error, a high probability exists that to a large extent the reader's views, your views, are based on falsehood! *Isn't this a scary thought?*

As Americans, we like to think that we are above all this. In America, *everybody is right*! It is an "I'm OK, You're OK" world. This is the new age, post-modernist, philosophy—a belief that truth is relative. Every set of beliefs is "true" for that believer. Dare to take a stand and claim to know a truth that implies another person is wrong, and you risk being labeled intolerant.

Nevertheless, a moment of rational thought disproves this comforting perspective. If Jesus existed, he existed. The issue is a question of history. If true, this truth is equal for the believer as well as the nonbeliever. If Mohammed was a prophet, then this is a true fact, regardless of who believes in it. Only a fanatic can maintain the dogmatic position that truth is relative.

Ah, but what about morals? Maybe, morality can be said to be relative to the individual or to cultures. Isn't morality a question of opinion that cannot be scientifically proven?

Even in terms of morals and ethics, however, absolute standards exist. Science is not the only method of acquiring knowledge. Logical deduction is also a valid method of discovery, and the argument for moral relativism cannot be logically maintained:

Consider for yourself, is there some moral issue that you are willing to take a stand on? Is there some moral standard that you are willing to say is an absolute, and anyone who crosses this line and violates this standard is morally reprehensible? Would you be willing to judge him or her as such?

This standard would cross cultural and national borders, so that even if someone was raised believing the opposite and acted on this indoctrinated belief, would you still be willing to condemn this person, or even the whole culture and society, as being morally degenerate and wrong?

You might be surprised to know how many people are unwilling to take a stand. So let's look at an issue and decide—is morality relative, or is there some absolute standard out there? *(The purpose of this discussion is not to define this standard, which admittedly is a problematic task. Rather, its purpose is to show that we all really do believe in absolute truth and absolute moral standards, despite the fact that we may differ with regard to what these standards are.)*

Almost all western societies agree that polygamy, the practice of taking multiple wives, is wrong. In fact, the polygamist leaders of fundamentalist Mormon sects in the western United States and Canada are often arrested for practicing this lifestyle. People professing the ideology of moral relativism likewise will agree that it is wrong—to them, in their opinion. However, they argue that they cannot force others to accept their point of view. In other words, they refuse to take a moral stand. Therefore, the moral relativist will not condemn, for example, a community of people in Africa or the Middle East who permit polygamy as a legitimate lifestyle.

However, when asked whether the existence of a sect of polygamists living isolated somewhere in the western United States should be allowed, the moral relativist admits that such a sect is unacceptable. Here, the moral relativist will distinguish immorality of the sect from the acts of the foreign community by responding that our society has declared polygamy as wrong, whereas the other culture has not.

This reasoning is patently flawed. The logical extension of arguing this position means that Nazi Germany was morally justified in exterminating its Jewish population, that Serbia was permitted to engage in ethnic cleansing, and that the Roman sport of throwing Christians to the lions was ethical. After all in each case, the relevant legal authority sanctioned the activity. Furthermore, this logic argues that the Nuremberg war tribunal acted immorally in bringing Nazis to justice, and that the Nuremberg judges should be condemned because they imposed their own moral standard on people, who acted rightly according to the rule of law of their culture and society.

Ironically, the outcome of this line of reasoning is the formulation of at least one absolute moral standard—that it is immoral to judge people in other cultures. Therefore, relativism is inherently contradictory. It, itself, is a radical position, and it drives people away from the search for truth.

If this is so, that truth is not relative, there has to be a way of arriving at "five-finger certainty" about our basic views on life. We must be able to discern a clear vision of reality, of who we are and the purpose of our existence, without becoming a fanatic.

Clarity and Conviction

Across the board, all over the world, everyone agrees: No matter who we are—the Pope, Fidel Castro, the Ayatollah, or the No Absolutes Philosophy Professor—we all subscribe to one idea: A person is capable of knowing truth. If that person searches diligently and sincerely, with the willingness to find the truth, it is within his or her grasp.

Indeed, most will even go so far as to say that everyone has an obligation to seek the truth. This message gets twisted, however,

Exercises~

❶ Take a stand! Make a list of values that you believe are universal to such a degree that you would morally condemn a person or society for violating them.

❷ A co-worker came to you to complain about her boss, because her boss just made a pass at her (nothing lewd, but your co-worker thinks that their professional relationship is now compromised). What advice do you give your friend? Do you support her position? If so, what gives you the moral right to say that the actions of her boss were wrong? Do you sympathize with the Boss (your friend is very attractive, single, and any heterosexual guy would want to ask her out on a date)? Can you do this and still support your friend?

❸ Watch the film *Judgment At Nuremberg*. Discuss and analyze the arguments presented.

because at the same time, people are also telegraphing the message that if you have not yet found truth, it is because you have not searched hard enough and, as a result, there is something morally reprehensible about you.

Imagine that you are a non-Christian, and you get a personal audience with the Pope. You ask him, "Is it really true that a non-Christian can't get into heaven no matter how good a life they lead unless they believe in Jesus?" The Pope might hum and haw a bit, but he would have to admit, this concept is a basic tenant of the theology of Christianity. If you were to then argue with him, claiming that it is not fair, he would respond, "Sure it's fair. If you were really searching for the truth, sincerely, honestly, and willing to change and to pay the price, then long ago you would have found that Jesus died to save you. You would then be able to get into heaven."

The same is true for the Christian who gets an audience with the Ayatollah. The scenario would be the same except that he would say, "If you were really searching for the truth, sincerely, honestly, and willing to change and to pay the price, you would have discovered long ago that no God exists but Allah and Mohammed is his prophet."

And, for the person who asks Fidel Castro, "What are my chances of going to heaven?" Fidel would respond, "Get off the opiate of the masses! Only communism can create paradise, and if you were seeking the truth sincerely, instead of trying to enrich yourself on the backs of the poor, you would see this."

Even the moral relativist university professor would have a similar answer. Imagine that someone accuses such a professor of undermining morality in the world and claims that there is a special place in the worst part of hell reserved for people espousing relativist philosophy. The professor might respond, "Look, the first thing you need to know is that there is no such place as hell. But if there were, it's people like you who would be frying there. It's fanatics like you that bring all kinds of discord into the world—religion has caused the worst of all human misery and suffering. Now if you had the courage to open your antediluvian head just a tiny crack, to allow the light of reason to penetrate that murk, then you would see that what I'm telling you is true—there is no absolute truth."

Of course, in this manner of thinking there is at least the absolute that there are no absolute truths. The professor must be espousing something; he must be teaching something. And if he does not believe in the absolute truth of his message, he is certainly a hypocrite.

Our daily lives are full of experiences that show us that we all believe that there is one right way. How many times have we been in arguments where we have had the thought, "If this guy would just be a little more open-minded, he would see that I'm right"? Anytime we have an argument with someone, *we are saying that there is a right way*—and therein lays our belief in truth. Otherwise, we would not be arguing.

All over the world, human beings agree on one thing: A person *can* know the truth. We all agree that if you search diligently and sincerely, with a willingness to pay the price, you will find the truth.

Not only this, but we all recognize that there are some truths that we already know with absolute clarity. We know certain facts are true; we all know that we have five-fingers on each hand. We also know that certain of our beliefs, certain aspects of our moral framework, are absolutely true. We have five-finger clarity that pedophilia is wrong and that murder is wrong.

Think about it! Knowledge of truth is attainable! The issue is whether we have attained it, whether all of our beliefs are true. By knowing what you know, you will be able to deduce whether what you believe in is the truth or not.

Exercises~

❶ Survey ten people and ask them whether or not truth is attainable.

❷ Choose a moral issue that you feel is wrong, and survey another ten people, asking them (a) whether they agree with you, (b) whether it is always wrong in all places and at all times, and (c) on what basis do they know that the answer they gave you is true.

Categorize Your Conviction

Absolute clarity is attainable, and there are areas of your knowledge base of which you have absolute confidence. You are one hundred percent certain of the fact that you have five fingers on each hand, and of some of your moral values. You do not have to hear all the different points of view before you conclude that you have five fingers or that murder is wrong. The fact that somebody out there may make a claim to the contrary, or that there are societies which do not seem to respect human life in the same way as you, does not diminish your clarity on these points.

Your knowledge base can be compared to a chain. Even a heavy steel chain is only as strong as its weakest link: One link of tin in the middle, and the chain is worthless. A shorter chain is inevitably better than a longer one with a tin link—at least it has some use.

The same holds true for your knowledge base. When your convictions are ironclad, they build you up as a human being and give you an identity. They give you strength of personality. Areas of confusion, on the other hand, weaken the strength of your persona. Therefore, you must identify the areas of confusion—the tin links in the chain of who you are. By identifying these areas of doubt, you learn what you are unclear about. This allows you to isolate and remove the areas of uncertainty—to strengthen your chain.

Isolating those areas of uncertainty prevents self-doubt from inhibiting you. It frees you to maintain strong convictions in other areas. It also provides you with the benefit of knowing where you need to strengthen your value systems through education.

The Four Categories of Conviction

All of convictions fit into one of four categories:

* *Knowledge:* You are absolutely sure that you are right (5 finger clarity; murder is wrong).

* *Belief:* You have evidence, but room for doubt continues to exist.

* *Faith:* You desire something to be true, but you have no substantive supporting evidence.

* *Socialization:* People have told you something, and you have accepted their veracity without serious independent investigation.

It is important to understand the differences between these four categories. Knowledge is absolute confidence—you know you have five fingers. You can see them and count them. Their number is unchanging. Others can see them and count them as well. You know others things, too, with complete confidence. You know that you did not rob a bank this week. You know murder is wrong. (It is a violation of the sanctity of human life; if permitted, it would cause society to fall apart, so you have plenty of logical points on which to pin you knowledge.)

On the other hand, are you sure that your brother did not rob a bank this week? You cannot know that with five-finger certainty. You have evidence of your brother's good character, but you cannot be absolutely sure. Your confidence in your brother's innocence is not knowledge; it is belief. If someone came with witnesses, fingerprints, and a video showing your brother walking into a bank with a gun saying, "Give me all your money," you would say, "Gee, I never would have believed it."

Faith is a leap beyond logic. Faith is a product of desire. Religious convictions are often based on faith. Have you ever gotten a stock market tip that was supposed to be guaranteed—you will make at least 50% profit, if not double or triple your money? People find these tips irresistible, because they want so badly to make money effortlessly. That is faith. In reality, we should have enough sense to give ourselves an education before taking the plunge.

Socialization covers all the ideas a person accepts as a member of a particular society. Society influences a person to accept certain assumptions. Chances are that you have not independently investigated all of what your society has taught you. In America, capitalism is right; in China, communism is right. In Italy, a person is likely to be a Catholic; in Iran, most people are Shiite Muslims. Accepting society's norms is not knowledge. It is following the crowd.

> We live in a real world, and we are constantly making judgments according to our convictions. It makes sense to know whether the convictions driving our actions are based on knowledge, belief, faith or socialization. It makes sense to know on what basis we are acting in order for us to judge how much known truth supports our behavior.

When a person wants to enter a business relationship with someone else, what information should be known? What level of investigation is required? Sometimes people enter into partnerships not because they have evidence to support their knowledge that their future partner is trustworthy, but because of their desire to believe their partner is trustworthy because of the promise of financial success. The consequences of such decisions can be life altering.

When a person wants to get married, what criteria should go into a proper choice of spouse? Many people are carried away by looks, but looks can be deceiving. When a company hires a CEO, they do a background check. Their investigation is called a due diligence review. Regarding the decision to get married on the other hand, people are swept away by romantic talk and the summer moon. The emotional desire for a fulfilling love relationship is so intense that people often make this vastly important decision based on faith, a desire to believe in the character of an intended spouse, rather than any substantive belief or knowledge. Is it any wonder that divorce rates in the U.S. exceed fifty percent?

Everything cannot be known with five-finger certainty. Sometimes you must to act on another basis. If you were sitting in a cafeteria and a friend yelled out that the cake contains poison, then your decision on whether or not to take a bite would have to be based on what you believe to be true. There is no time to do a spectrograph analysis.

In such situations, you would not need absolute clarity to make a decision. However, with regard to the most critical decisions you make in life—whom to marry, with whom to form a business venture, for what to give your life—doesn't it make sense to try to root these decisions in knowledge? Without question, by knowing what you know, by understanding why and on what basis you are making decisions, you will become a more confident and more rational human being. You will be a better decision maker.

Take the Test

The following list of statements will help you make sense of your current set of convictions. The first step is to ask yourself whether you think a particular statement, in your view, is true or false. Then specify in which of the four categories it belongs. Are there any that do not fit into any of the categories? Do this exercise individually and then try it with some friends.

K: Knowledge   B: Belief   F: Faith   S: Socialization

1. The world is round.
   T F   K B S F

2. Rich people are necessarily happier than poor people.
   T F   K B S F

3. Going to college helps people understand what they want out of life.
   T F   K B S F

4. It is likely that most people's beliefs and ideas come from their societies.
   T F   K B S F

5. A supreme being exists.
   T F   K B S F

6. Chocolate ice cream is better than vanilla.
   T F   K B S F

7. Edinburgh is the capital of England.
   T F   K B S F

8. Women are more intuitive than men.
   T F   K B S F

9. My mother loves me.
   T F   K B S F

10. Democracy is superior to communism
    T F   K B S F

11. People are basically good.
    T F   K B S F

12. All children can learn.
    T F   K B S F

13. Capital punishment is a deterrent to murder.
    T F   K B S F

14. There is no life after death.
    T F   K B S F

15. Scientists are objective.
    T F   K B S F

16. The Republican Party understands the free market system better than the Democrats.
    T F   K B S F

17. Many of my ideas and opinions come from my society.
    T F   K B S F

18. Corporal punishment should be allowed in schools.
    T F   K B S F

19. America is the best place in the world to live.
    T F   K B S F

20. It is wrong to steal.
    T F   K B S F

21. Taking home a package of computer paper from one's workplace is not stealing.
    T F   K B S F

22. Stress affects the health of one's body.
    T F   K B S F

23. Citizens have the right to bear arms.
    T F   K B S F

24. Stealing is illegal.
    T F   K B S F

25. If you don't know what you would be willing to die for, you don't know what to live for.
    T F   K B S F

26. Evolution is a more reasonable explanation for the origin of the universe than the Biblical account.
    T F   K B S F

27. If you are kind and patient with others, they are less likely to be rude to you.
    T F   K B S F

28. Canada is the second largest country in the world.
    T F   K B S F

29. Smoking causes lung cancer.
    T F   K B S F

30. There are several qualitatively different classes of pleasure available in this world
    T F   K B S F

31. An intellectual is one who makes decisions based on facts rather than emotions.
    T F   K B S F

32. We need to have goals in learning to get the most out of our learning time.
    T F   K B S F

33. There is no such thing as free will.
    T F   K B S F

Putting It All Together

You began this journey by learning that there are four self-evident ground rules to life:

✳ People acquire knowledge and beliefs to the extent that they accept information conveyed to them as being true, and this knowledge and these beliefs determine who a person is and how they behave. Therefore, all students of life— all people—are responsible for critically analyzing information obtained. People must investigate and judge the validity of anything they are told or hear.

✳ There is ultimately only one motivating factor to all decision-making—pleasure.

✳ The root of all problems is mistaking things as pleasurable, which are not.

✳ The ultimate mistake is not taking the responsibility to get an education—not to investigate what life is all about; to understand what provides life's greatest pleasures and how these are obtained.

You then went on to learn that there are five levels of categorically different types of pleasure available in this world:

✳ **PHYSICAL PLEASURE**
   The price is physical exertion
   The counterfeit is self-indulgence and comfort

✳ **LOVE (Relationships)**
   The price is commitment
   The counterfeit is lust

✳ **MEANING (Goodness)**
   The price is courage
   The counterfeit is social pressure—looking good rather than being good

✳ **CREATIVITY (The *power* to create life and give pleasure to others)**
   The price is responsibility
   The counterfeit is control and manipulation

✳ **AWE (The transcendental experience—sensing the interconnectedness of existence and your place in the infinite scheme of reality)**
   The price is humility
   The counterfeit is arrogance and self-absorption

Having learned about the pleasures available to a person, you then began to analyze how to choose effectively among them. You learned that the battle of life is activating your free will. Choice is a

constant endeavor, and the primary choice is essentially between life
and death, between the struggle to grow and the desire for comfort
and avoidance of pain. The ultimate choice is constant growth. The
five steps to choosing effectively are:

* **Awareness** (don't sleepwalk through life).

* **Independence**, which implies three things: *freedom from
externally and internally defined preconceived notions*—from
society and from one's own past (one cannot be trapped by
how others view one or by one's own past); *self-knowledge*
(people suffer from cognitive dissonance); and *responsibility*
(only you make your choices, you are responsible for them,
and you have the power to change). Start each day anew.

* **Beware aware** of the body-soul conflict.

* **Identify** with the soul and raise your level of choice. This
leads to inner peace.

* **Direct** self-growth and reach beyond self.

Next, you looked into the process of directing your self-growth,
which in essence is how free will is manifest in one area of the
human condition. It is a process that develops the trait of integrity,
and we called this process the five belts to being an intellectual:

* **The WHITE BELT is definitions:** *You cannot achieve any-
thing without defined goals*

* **The ORANGE BELT is saying what you mean:** *You
must use your definitions.*

* **The RED BELT is meaning what you say:** *You need to
connect your emotions to your intellect.*

* **The BROWN BELT is living with what you mean:**
*Apply it:think before you act, plan your day, and plan your life
(know what you are living for).*

✳ **The BLACK BELT is unification:** *Develop a constant awareness of the connection between your actions and your life plan (live your ideal life 24 hours a day) and by doing so allow your vision to expand beyond self.*

Finally, having understood that it all comes down to pleasure, having defined pleasure, having learned to how to choose, and how to direct your self-growth, you investigated how to know that you have made the right choices. You saw that people are generally not secure in their convictions, and that they are subject to outside pressure and to the whims of society, and that the key to a secure and confident life is striving to "know what you know." In this discussion, you learned that all convictions fall into four categories—knowledge, belief, faith, and socialization. Obviously, you should strive to base your critical choices on convictions rooted in knowledge, in five-finger clarity of their truthfulness.

Tools of Living

This book has been all about accessing the tools of living. And with the power of these tools comes responsibility—to yourself and to others.

Now, reviewing all that you have learned, it is time to ask, was the journey worth it? Apply the principles learned in this last chapter to this book as a whole and ask yourself these questions:

✳ Are the major principles conveyed in this book true or false?

✳ How do you know your answer to be true?

✳ Is your answer based on knowledge, belief, faith, or socialization?

If you conclude that the points made in this book are true, you've got to consider how they change the way you look at life. Are there any implications for your behavior? Can you integrate and implement anything new that you have learned?

That's how you can take these lessons and run with them. As we've discussed, unlike other creations, we humans have free will. Within this divine spark lies your potential to shape and change both your inner world and the world around you.

It Takes Practice

I could explain to you in exactly five minutes how to play tennis, but do you think you're going to be good at it? It's going to take practice, even if you're talented. The same goes for baseball, the martial arts, dance, gymnastics, musical performance, yoga or any other discipline. It takes many hours, even years, to become a master.

Yes, it takes practice. So think it through…literally. Get a grip on yourself. Know yourself, be true to yourself and it follows that as night follow day, you will reach your goals.

You live in a universe filled with possibilities, and you have made a conscious decision to push forward.

You have learned how to enjoy the higher classes of pleasure; you've taken those life-tasting lessons. When you accustom yourself to doing this, then you will truly be able to say, "Life is giving me everything I want and more."

appendix
Going Further *with* Suggested Readings

You can dig even deeper into each of the concepts presented in this book by taking some time to reviewing key passages from the following books.

CHAPTER 1

The Bible, Chapters 1:1 to 2:24
The idea exists in the Judeo-Christian worldview that all humanity is descendent from a single human being. Reading these passages, does the concept of a single progenitor necessarily mean that all of humanity today shares certain traits of decision-making? If we are decedent from primates, would this fact weaken the idea that decision-making is governed by certain common principles? Is the science of psychology based on a similar idea that certain principles govern the path to a happy life and an ethical life?

Gray, Peter. *Psychology, 2nd Ed.* Worth Publishers (New York, 1994). Chapter 1—"The History and Scope of Psychology," pp. 3-23.
This introduction to psychology provides an overview of the views and trends in psychology. Consider whether the concept of psychology as a science presupposes the existence of, and an ability to measure, universal principles (or rules) governing emotion and behavior. If so, doesn't this also mean that the elements of a happy life and of good decision-making are universal among human beings and can be studied and learned?

Cosmidos, Leda and Tooby, John. *Evolutionary Pychology: A Primer.* Center for Evolutionary Psychology. (www.psych.ucsb.edu/research/cep/primer.html)
Consider whether evolutionary psychology is based on the notion that humanity as a whole has developed a common set of emotion and decision-making patterns necessary for survival over the millennium. Furthermore, consider whether evolutionary psychologists would argue that there is optimal emotional reaction to any given circumstance, which should somehow be measurable?

Brown, Donald E. *Human Universals.* Temple University Press (Philadelphia, 1991). "Introduction," pp. 1-7.
Brown argues that though anthropology generally focuses on the cultural variances among peoples, in reality those differences tend to be superficial and are far outweighed by universally held similarities.

Kant, Immanuel. *Foundations of the Metaphysics of Morals*, Beck, Lewis White, trans. The Bobbs-Merrill Company, Inc. (Indianapolis, 1969). "Preface," pp. 3-10.
Central to the approach of philosophy to understanding concepts of morality is the idea that standards of morality transcend an individual's particular circumstances and must meet some ultimate standard of behavior. This idea is well-expressed by Kant, who asserts that a moral law must be a priori (one which derives from a premise rather than from empirical data). By definition, morality transcends individual perception, which is the individual's greatest challenge, "For man is affected by so many inclinations that, though he is capable of the idea of a practical pure person, he is not so easily able to make it concertedly effect the conduct of this life." (p. 6.)

Mill, John Stuart. *Utilitarianism, Liberty and Representative Government.* J.M. Dent & Sons, Ltd (London, 1940). "Utilitarianism"—Chapter 1, pp. 1-5, and Chapter 5, pp. 38-60.
Mill, too, acknowledges that principles of morality must transcend the individual, "...morality of an individual's action is not a question of direct perception, but the application of a law to an individual case." And this standard is a universal one, "We do not call anything wrong unless we mean to imply a person aught to be punished in some way or other for doing it."

Lear, Jonathan. Brown, S.C., ed. *Objectivity and Cultural Divergence.* Cambridge University Press (Cambridge, 1984). pp. 135-176.
Considering the influence of culture on our value system, are we free morally? If so, on what basis can we set a standard?

Spradley, James P. and McCurdy, David W. "Culture and the Contemporary World." Spradley, James P. and McCurdy, David W, eds. *Conformity and Conflict: Readings in Cultural Anthropology, 5th ed.* Little, Brown & Co. (Boston, 1984). pp. 1-11.
This article presents a good overview of the power of values in controlling a person's actions. It ends with a discussion of multiculturalism. Do you see a contradiction between the authors' criticism of traditional "values," such as concepts of male superiority, demands that inner city children learn only "proper English," and the suppression of Indian culture, and the authors' call to our society to "relinquish those values with destructive consequences"? Might it not be argued that concepts of male superior have been effective social regulators for thousands of years, or that forcing minorities to adopt "proper English" is an effective method of integrating new citizens into mainstream society? In your opinion, who should decide which values a society decides to promote through its laws?

Milgram, Stanley. *Obedience to Authority: An Experimental View.* Harper & Row Publishers (New York, 1974).
Read Chapter 1, pp. 1-12 and the Epilogue, pp. 179-189. Do you think that the participants in Dr. Milgram's experiments or the soldiers would have acted differently had they had a clear conception of their own value system prior to the critical events?

CHAPTER 2

Maslow, Abraham H. *Motivation and Personality.* Harper & Row. (New York, 1970). "A Theory of Human Motivation," pp. 35-58.
Maslow sets out a theory of human motivation based on a hierarchy of needs, wherein he posits that people are initially driven to satisfy "lower" needs, which

when satisfied, lead a person to pursuing successively "higher" needs. Maslow's hierarchy progresses as follows: physiological needs (food and water), safety needs (clothes and shelter), belonging (love and relationships), self-esteem, and self-actualization. Consider how this hierarchy may be consistent with the concept of a hierarchy of pleasures. Consider whether there might still be a level of need, which surpasses self-actualization. If there is, what could it be?

Dewey, John. *Theory of The Moral Life.* **Holt, Rinehart & Winston. (New York 1960). pp. 43-44**
In this passage, Dewey seems to agree that qualitatively distinct levels of pleasure exist. Do you agree with Dewey that what distinguishes one class of pleasure from another is that a higher class of pleasure is one which "bear reflecting upon"? What type of experience would be one that unifies "in a harmonious way his whole system of desires"?

Peck, M. Scott, MD. *The Road Less Traveled.* **Simon & Schuster (New York, 1978). "Problems and Pain" and "Delaying Gratification," pp. 15-19.**
Peck states that "life is difficult" and the failure to accept this fact is a primary source of psychological problems. The key to success is discipline and that the undisciplined trait of problem avoidance results in neurosis. Peck shows that a paradoxical relationship exists between discipline and procrastination, wherein avoiding the pain of responsible decision causes a greater level of pain in the long-run. Consider whether the discussion of pain being the price of pleasure and pleasure being maximized as a result of focus is consistent with Peck's views.

McCarthy, Ed, and Ewing-Mulligan, Mary. *Wine for Dummies.* **John Wiley & Sons, Inc. (Hoboken, NJ, 2006). Chapter Two—"These Taste Buds are for You," pp. 19-24.**
Becoming a connoisseur takes effort. Concentrate on how the authors of this wine-tasting book describe how one learns to take pleasure in an experience.

Okakura, Kakuzo. *The Book of Tea.* **Kodansha International (Tokyo, 1989). "Schools of Tea," pp. 43-54.**
In this classic work about the Japanese Tea Ceremony, Okakura describes how a society of aficionados has turned the drinking of a beverage into a "religion of aestheticism." (p. 29)

Hobbs, Thomas. "Of Liberty." Molesworth, Sir William, ed. *The English Works of Thomas Hobbes, vol. II.* **Bart, John Bohn (Covent Garden, 1966). Chapter 1, pp 1-13.**
The view that man is driven by self-interest is often referred to as a Hobbesian view of human nature. In this reading, Hobbes clearly describes man as motivated by his own self-preservation.

Hume, David. *Enquiry Concerning the Principles of Morals*, **Beauchamp, Tom L. ed. Clarendon Press (Oxford, 1998). Appendix 2—"On Self-Love," pp. 90-95.**
In this selection, Hume outlines five of the major arguments against the concept of psychological egoism. Do you find the arguments persuasive?

Feinberg, Joel. "Psychological Egoism." Feinberg, Joel and Shaffer-Landau, Russ, eds. *Reason & Responsibility*, **10ᵗʰ ed. Wadsworth Publishing Company (Belmont, 1999). pp. 493-506.**
In this article Feinberg attempts to refute the validity of Psychological Egoism. In his example about President Lincoln saving a group of little pigs, Feinberg asserts

that Lincoln had a pre-existing desire for something other than his own happiness. This, he argues, proves that Lincoln did not save the pigs out of his self-interest in his own happiness. In reading this part of the essay, consider whether Feinberg is confusing the concepts of pleasure, happiness, and self-interest. Consider what distinguished Lincoln from his fellow passenger, who did not care to save the pigs. Consider whether Lincoln would have been motivated to save the pigs if he would not have received any satisfaction from the act (like his fellow passenger). Is it possible that an external factor could have motivated Lincoln to act, as Feinberg would suggest in the way he defines altruist behavior? Or, was Lincoln motivated by something intrinsic to his personality, and if so, how would you define that something?

Morton, Adam. *Disasters and Dilemmas: Strategies for Real-life Decision Making.* Basil Blackwell Ltd. (Oxford, 1991). Chapter 11:2—"The Aging Addict," pp 165-166 and Chapter 11:3—"Sila Marner meets Pere Goriot," pp. 166-167. In these essays Morton shows how self-interest is a poor descriptor of what motivates human action. Consider whether the drive for pleasure would more accurately explain the behavior of the characters in Morton's scenarios.

Marillo, Carolyn R. "The Reward Event & Motivation." *The Journal of Philosophy,* Vol. 87:4, April 1990, pp. 169-186. Applying data from psychological experiments and empirical arguments, Marillo shows that behavior is motivated by a "reward event," a physiological event in the brain. In lay parlance, wouldn't we call this reward event that Marillo describes intense "pleasure"?

Nagel, Thomas. *Mortal Questions.* Cambridge University Press (Cambridge, 1979). "Moral Luck," pp. 24-38. In this essay, Nagel demonstrates that people often judge the morality of an act in accordance with its results (sometimes the ends justify the means), even though these results are often only a matter of luck. Furthermore, Nagel points out that many other factors bearing on the morality, such as our individual circumstances and our moral outlook, are a matter of luck. With these arguments in mind, consider again the relative positions of Steve Brown and President George Bush, Jr. Is there a moral difference between the two of them? If not, on what basis does society have a right to send Brown to jail and to elect Bush to be president? If so, on what basis do you distinguish the two? Is it true, that ultimately, we are only judged in accordance with results? What are the implications of this to your daily life?

Plous, Scott. *The Psychology of Judgment and Decision Making.* Temple University Press (Philadelphia, 1993). Chapter 21—"Behavioral Traps," pp. 241-252. In this chapter, Plous lists a number of common thought patterns, which results in mistaken judgments. These "traps" cause people to miscalculate which path among a person's various options will lead to the most pleasurable result.

Morton, Adam. *Disasters and Dilemmas: Strategies for Real-life Decision Making.* Basil Blackwell Ltd. (Oxford, 1991). Chapters 1—"Patterns of Desire," pp. 3-12. Morton discusses the thought patterns, which go into good and bad decision-making. If we substitute the phrase "the Drive for Pleasure" in place of Morton's use of the term "Desire" would we attain a clearer understanding of human decision-making?

Aristotle. *Nicomachean Ethics,* Terence, Irwin, trans. Hackett Publishing Company, Inc. (Indianapolis, 1999). Book II, Chapter 3—"[The Importance of Pleasure and Pain]," pp. 20-21.
The role of pleasure and pain as a primary motivation forces in decision making was well-recognized by Aristotle. Likewise, Aristotle recognized that misconceptions about pain and pleasure cause misfortune, and thus, people need an education with regard to what is truly pleasurable: "For pleasure causes us to do base actions, and pain causes us to abstain from fine ones. That is why we need to have had the appropriate upbringing—right from early youth, as Plato says—to make us find enjoyment or pain in the right things; for this is the correct education."

Patterson, David. *When Learned Men Murder.* Phi Delta Kappa (Bloomington, 1996), "Introduction," pp. 1-6, and "When Learned Men Murdered: Implications of the Wannsee Conference for Higher Education," pp. 7-27.
Is there anything in higher education, which is inconsistent with murder? Or, after all is said and done and taught and learned, can we not expect the products of our university to be no more moral than at the beginning of the process?

The Complete Garlic Lovers' Cookbook. Celestial Arts (Berkeley, 1987). "The Festival," pp. 5-6.
Does your mouth water at the description of all the gastronomic delights available at the Festival? Are you amazed the array of sensory experiences available in one simple spice?

Keller, Helen. *The Story of My Life.* Double Day & Company, Inc. (Garden City, 1905). "Introduction" by Perry, Ralph Barton, pp. 13-17.
Helen Keller represents the triumph of the human spirit over adversity. Her life and accomplishments are no less than awe-inspiring. Try to imagine for a moment suffering with her challenges. Think about the quality of life that you would have. Now, consider that Ms. Keller almost never complained and lived an exceptionally fulfilled life by her own account. Does reading about her story give you a greater appreciation for the gifts that you were born with? Does considering her life make you reconsider you would ever recommend a therapeutic abortion based on in utero testing?

Rubenstein, Samuel. "Asceticism: Christian Perspectives." Johnston, William M., ed. *Encyclopedia of Monasticism,* Vol. 1. Fitzroy, Dearborn Publishers (Chicago, 2000). pp. 92-94.
Do you believe that living an ascetic life can lead one to a more spiritual existence? If so, do you think that the trade-off is worth it?

Brandt, Richard. "Hedonism." Edwards, Paul, ed. *The Encyclopedia of Philosophy,* Vol. 3 & 4. MacMillam Publishing Co., Inc. & The Free Press (New York, 1967). pp. 432-435.
To what degree do you think that the arguments set forth so far in this textbook are hedonistic? Assume for the moment that there is no G-d; can you present an argument as to why the pursuit of material and physical pleasure should not be the ultimate goal of your existence?

Kayser, Karen. *When Love Dies: The Process of Marital Disaffection.* The Guilford Press (New York, 1993). "Love in Contemporary Marriage," "The Transition to a Love-Centered Marriage," and "The Concept of Marital Disaffection," pp. 1-8.
These passages describe how marriages fail, when they do not meet the expecta-

tions of their spouses. These expectations are a sense happiness and self-fulfillment, which Kayser equates with the sense of love that marriage partners desire to feel. Disaffection results when these "needs" are not met, leading to a dissipation of the loving feelings, which originally brought the couple together. Stated another way, relationships exist to provide their partners, each individually and personally, with a very essential pleasurable experience. When the relationship ceases to provide this pleasure, the relationship ceases. Marriages fall apart when the effort required to maintain them no longer provides the desired reward. Toward the end of the book, the author describes different types of exercises, different types of effort, which partners can engage in that are designed to result in the pleasure that both are seeking and which is required to build a positive relationship.

Kennedy, John F. *Profiles in Courage.* Harper & Row Publishers (New York, 1964). "Courage and Politics," pp. 21-41.
Kennedy describes in his introduction to this book the various pressures restricting a Senator's ability to follow his conscience on every vote. Courage is thus defined as the strength of will to rise above these pressures and risk the negative consequences. Think about what equivalent pressures bear on our everyday lives, and how often we subjugate our true will to such outside pressures.

Eliach, Yaffa. *Hasidic Tales of the Holocaust.* Vintage Books (New York, 1988). "Even the Transgressors in Israel," pp. 155-159.
In this true and moving story of courage of people who knew what to live for and what to die for, a group of prisoners are willing to risk death to maintain their beliefs. Nevertheless, what touches the soul on the deepest level is the action of foreman, who though long ago gave up his faith, realized in an instant that his own goodness and self-respect are necessary to his existence.

Woodward, Bob. *Wired: The Short Life and Fast Times of John Belushi.* Simon and Shuster (New York, 1984). pp. 15-22.
The opening pages of this biography of one funniest and most popular comedians of the latter half of the 20th century describe a man of the fast track to a drug overdose. Think about what could drive a person, seemingly on top of the world, to engage in such self-destructive behavior. Think about his statement to actress Carrie Fischer in the midst of this binge, "This can't be it. This can't be all of it. This isn't enough. There has to be more, something else!" What is he lacking?

Kavka, Gregory S. "The Reconciliation Project." Zimmerman, David and Copp, David, eds. *Morality, Reason, and Truth.* Rowman & Allanheld (Totowa, 1985). pp. 297-319.
In this essay, Kafka attempts to reconcile what he classifies as one of the oldest problems of moral philosophy, namely the relationship between ethical behavior and self-interest. The reader must note that Kafka's starting point is that these two concepts—morality and self-interest—are in inherent conflict. Additionally, Kafka views the concept meaning as an external overlay on individual psyche as opposed to something intrinsically part of it, "The most promising such device is an appeal to our need to give meaning to our lives and endeavors" [emphasis added]. Meaning is an artificial concept in Kafka's view.

The argument of this lesson is that humanity has an intrinsic drive toward goodness and meaning as these qualities provide us with a most exquisite, and indeed necessary, pleasure. Therefore, there can be no conflict between ethical behavior and self-interest; Kafka's paradigm is misplaced. Moreover, since we have a drive toward goodness (though we are often misled), the search for meaning in our lives, which provides this pleasure, must be an expression of our internal essence. Meaning is not an artificial façade that we place over our actions in order to facilitate our interaction with the world around us!

In reviewing this essay, consider which view is more accurate—Kafka's or ours?

D'este, Carlo. Patton: A Genius for War. Harper Perennial (New York, 1995). "Patton of course: The Battle of the Bulge," pp. 674-682.
Patton was a great believer in destiny. He lived his whole life with a view to one day leading the greatest force ever assembled into the greatest battle. His study and understanding of warfare was unmatched by any of his contemporaries. His preparedness was also unmatched. Imagine his pleasure at the meeting of the Allied General Staff described here, as he was about to take responsibility for the fulfillment of his destiny.

Chandler, David P. *Brother Number One: A Political Biography of Pol Pot*, revised edition. Westview Press (Boulder, 1999). pp. 1-5 & 180-188.
The leaders of the communistic insurgency in Cambodia attempted to impose on their nation a complete restructuring of society. They forcibly moved peasants to the cities and city dwellers to the country, and they outlawed currency. The human cost of this endeavor was hundreds of thousands of lives. Consider what possessed the leadership to attempt such a revolution; consider what type of utopia you would attempt to create if you were given the means to do so. What costs would you exact? Think about what the Pol Pot, the leader of this revolution could have been like as a person. Indeed, Chandler notes that he had a thirst for power. Imagine the pleasure he got from being Brother Number One. Also note that despite the human cost, even his enemies viewed Pol Pot as congenial; he did not exhibit the tyrannical ravings that we like to associate with despots. Does this trouble you?

Maslow, Abraham. "The 'Core-religious,' or 'Transcendental,' Experience." *Religion, Values, and Peak Experiences.* **Ohio State University Press (Columbus, 1964). Reprinted in: White, John, ed. *The Highest State of Consciousness* (Garden City, 1972). pp. 352-364.**
Maslow describes all "peak" experiences as expressions of the same phenomenon. Carefully view his list of common descriptions of such experiences, particularly how people describe a feeling of wholeness as resulting from such experiences. Are peak experiences and awe experiences synonymous?

Watts, Alan W. *This Is It and Other Essays on Zen and Spiritual Experiences.* Collier Books (New York, 1970). "This Is It," pp. 19-40.
Consider how Watts describes the ultimate experience.

CHAPTER 3

Wynne, Clive. "Do Animals Think? The Case Against the Animal Mind" and Griffin, Donald. "How Human is Enough: A Response." *Psychology Today,* **Vol. 32, November/December 1999, pp. 50-53.**
Can you articulate what distinquishes human choice from animal choice? Whast separates man from animal? Is the distinction one of quantity or one of quality?

Hitler, Adolf. *Mein Kompf*, Munhein, Ralph, trans. Houghton Mifflim Company (Boston, 1971). pp. 327-330.
Consider the arguments by which Hitler justified a policy of racial purity. Do you think he thought he was trying to achieve a higher good?

Mandela, Nelson. *Long Walk to Free: The Autobiography of Nelson Mandela.* Little, Brown and Company (Boston, 1994). Chapter 115—"Freedom," pp. 543-544.

Nelson Mandela spent 27 and a half years in prison because he dared to struggle for freedom. After reading this passage, consider how Mandela defines of freedom. Note how he uses the expressions "freedom to" and "freedom from."

Frankl, Victor E. *Man's Search for Meaning.* Washington Square Press (New York, 1984). pp. 95-101.

In these passages, Frankl vivdly describes how hope and meaning are necessary to life, and how they enable a person to survive the most harrowing situations. He shows how a person's inner life can free a person and elvate them beyond their present circumstances. He also describes how a person's life will disintegrate without a sense of meaning and how finding this meaning is necessary to bring a person back from the edge of suicide.

Maltsberger, John T. "The Pychodynamic of Understanding Suicide." Jacobs, Douglas G., ed. *The Harvard Medical School Guide to Suicide Assessment and Intervention.* Jossey-Bass Publishers (San Francisco, 1999). pp. 72-82 (alternatively, pp. 72-73, 82).

Consider whether the Harvard Medical School Guide's discussion of suicide in this chapter is consistent with the observations of Victor Frankl.

Freud, Sigmund. *The Ego and the Id*, Riviere, Joan, trans., Strachey, James, ed. WW Norton & Company, Inc. (New York, 1962). Chapter IV—"The Two Classes of Instincts," pp. 30-32.

Can Freud's view of the human psyche be understood as consistent with a deterministic view of free will?

Rand, Ayn. *The Virtue of Selfishness.* New American Library (New York, 1964). "The Objectivists Ethics," pp. 13-17.

Rand asks the questions whether morality really exists or whether good and evil are completely subjective. In her quest for an answer she observes, "There only one fundemental alterntive is the universe: existence and nonexistence." Clearly, Rand sees the tension between life and death as not only the lynchpin for free will, but for defining good and evil as well.

Campbell, C.A. *In Defense of Free Will and Other Essays.* George Allen & Vuunin Ltd. (London, 1967). Chapter II—"In Defense of Free Will," pp. 35-55.

Campbell points out that the discussion of free will is essential to the concept of personal responsibility. He represents the libertarian point of view that two criteria must be met for free will to exist: Man must be the sole cause of his choice—he must have self-determination; and man could have exerted his causality in an alternative way—he could have acted differently. Consider whether he accurately addresses when choices actually result from free will, and what characterizes these moments.

Hogarth, Robin. *Judgement and Choice.* John Wiley & Sons (Chichester, 1987). Chapter 1—"The Nature of Human Judgement," pp. 1-10.

This chapter provides a nice overview on how the mind works. Note the different ways that decisions are often made without active thinking, e.g. heuristics.

Rand, Ayn. *The Virtue of Selfishness*. New American Library (New York, 1964). "The Objectivists Ethics," pp. 13-17.

Rand asserts that one's range of action is proportionate to one's level of consciousness. She further argues that of all creations, man is the only one is which consciousness is volitional. Do you agree?

Fromm, Eric. *The Art of Being*. Continuum (New York, 1992). Chapters 7— "To Be Awake" and Chapter 8—"To Be Aware," pp. 33-44.

Note how Fromm describes the ways in which people can limit or expand their awakeness and awareness.

The Declaration of Independence and the *Gettysburg Address*.

Try to identify the elements of freedom and independence as exemplified in these documents. Are they contradictory insomuch as the South could be portrayed as seeking the same type of independence formerly sought by the founding fathers and Lincoln likened to King George? Can you find a distinction?

Plous, Scott. *The Psychology of Judgment and Decision Making*. Temple University Press (Philadelphia, 1993). Chapter 1—"Selective Perception," and Chapter 2—"Cognitive Dissonance," pp. 15-30.

In Chapter 1, Scott Plous provides an excellent overview of the ways in which preconceived notions and expectations color one's view of reality. Likewise, in Chapter 2, he nicely summarizes the effects of cognitive dissonance.

Shaffer, Jerome. *Philosophy of Mind*. Prentice-Hall, Inc. (Englewood Cliffs, 1968). "The Subject of Consciousness," pp. 34-59.

In this excerpt, Shaffer gives a thorough overview of various philosophical approaches to understanding the mind-body (body-soul) dynamic. Which approach seems most plausible to you? Does that approach support or contradict the concepts put forth in this lesson.

Lopiansky, Ahron. "The Human Core: Lessons from the Andrea Yates Killings." Aish HaTorah (Jerusalem, 2001). http://aish.com/societyWork/society/The_Human_Core.asp.

After physicality, memory and mental agility, and moral conscience are stripped away, what is left that can be called the person? What is the real you?

Kidder, Rushworth. *How Good People Make Tough Choices*. Simon & Schuster (New York, 1996). Chapter One—"Overview: The Ethics of Right versus Right," pp. 13-29.

Kidder describes the tough choices in life as those between right versus right, whereas questions of right versus wrong are mere moral temptations. Do you find his arguments compelling?

Watson, David L. and Tharp, Roland G. *Self-Directed Behavior: Self-Modification for Personal Adjustment*. Brooks/Cole Publishing Company (Monterey, 1972). "A Case History of Self-Modification" and "Your own Self-Modification Project—Step One," pp. 4-6, and "Self-Modification of Behavior," pp. 47-57.

What limits do you see to the method of behavioral change outlined in this reading? What types of behavior do you believe this method would be effective at changing? What types of behavior do you believe this method would be ineffective at changing?

Dewey, John. *Theory of a Moral Life.* Holt, Rinehart and Winston (New York, 1960). Chapter VI, Section 5—"The Moral Self: Responsibility and Freedom," pp. 168-174.
Consider how close Dewey's philosophy as set forth in this reading summarizes the concepts of free will discussed throughout this chapter.

Dunlap, Knight. *Habits, Their Making and Unmaking.* Liveright, Inc. (New York, 1932). Chapter 1—"The Problems of Habit and Learning," pp. 3-17.
This reading provides a solid overview of how habits are formed and the effect that they have on our personality. Dunlap observes, "A definite process of learning is the formation of habit; and conversely, a habit is a way of living that has been learned... Habits, in their totality, make up the character of the individual; that is, they are the individual, as the individual appears to other people." What do you think that Dunlap means when he says, "as the individual appears to other people"?

CHAPTER 4

Nathanson, Stephen. *The Ideal of Rationality: A Defense within Reason.* Open Court (Chicago, 1994). Chapter 1—"The Classical Ideal," pp. 3-12.
This reading presents the classic view that reason should dominate emotions and that rationalism should control one's actions. Notice though that even Socrates is passionate in his quest for truth, and this emotion drives his behavior.

Rand, Ayn. *The Virtue of Selfishness.* New American Library (New York, 1964). pp. 25-26.
Do you agree with Rand's statement, "Rationality is man's basic virtue, the source of all his other virtue. Man's basic vice, the source of all his evils is act of unfocusing his mind, the suspension of his consciousness..."?

Viscott, David. *The Language of Feeling.* Pocket Books (New York, 1976). pp 19-34.
Viscott presents the view that emotions, rather than intellectual thought, are what makes for healthy decision-making. Notice though how Viscott describes the necessity of understanding and controlling one's emotions. Is this not a rational activity?

Goleman, Daniel. *Emotional Intelligence.* Bantam Books (New York, 1995). Chapter 3—"When Smart is Dumb," pp. 33-36.
Goleman points out that human intelligence has many facets, only one of which is represented by IQ. In additional, people have emotional intelligence, which is often a better gauge of the chances for success in life, and which is characterized an ability to control one's emotions. Emotional intelligence is reflected one's ability to be self-motivated, to persist through adversity, to control impulses, to delay gratification, to regulate moods, to empathize, and so on. Goleman stresses that emotional intelligence can be learned, that it is a matter of skill. This lesson asserts that an intellectual is a person with a high level of emotional intelligence.

Polanyi, Michael. *Personal Knowledge: Towards A Post-Critical Philosophy.* University of Chicago Press (Chicago, 1962). "Intellectual passions," pp. 171-174.
What are your intellectual passions?

Martin, Mike W. *Self-Deception and Morality.* University Press of Kansas (Lawrence, 1986). Chapter 2—"Evading Self Acknowledgment," pp. 6-30.
This selection provides a good overview of various ways that people come to

deceive themselves. When reading it, consider the connection between subjective desire and self-deception. After reading it, reconsider you answer to the Food For Thought question about what you should do if your friend has a drug problem, but won't recognize it.

Perloff, Richard M. *The Dynamics of Persuasion*. Lawrence Erlbaum Associates, Publishers (Hillsdale, NJ, 1993). Chapter 4—"Attitudes and Behavior," pp. 78-104.
This selection provides an overview of the research done on the effect of attitudes on predicting behavior. Does this research support or contradict the ideas presented in this chapter? Perloff notes that attitudes are more likely to effect behavior when a person is in touch with their feelings. If this is true, doesn't it stand to reason that a person will only be guided by their purported morals and values only to the degree that they truly integrate these abstract concepts into their emotional being? Otherwise, their behavior is likely to be valueless. Do you agree?

Covey, Stephen R. *The Seven Habits of Highly Effective People: Powerful Lessons in Personal Change*. A Fireside Book, Simon & Schuster (New York, 1990). "Habit 3—Put First Things First: The Principles of Personal Management," pp. 145-182.
How do you manage your time? Which of Covey's four generations of time management do you use? Covey describes four quadrants of activities, which take up a person's time. How well does this describe your day?

Bolles, Richard Nelson. *What Color Is Your Parachute: A Practical Manual for Job-Hunters and Career-Changers*, 2001 Ed. Ten Speed Press (Berkeley. 2001). "Epilogue—How To Find Your Mission In Life," pp. 239-258.
Do you agree with Bolles' conception of the concept of "mission"? Can you articulate what your mission in life is?

CHAPTER 5

Hunter, Edward. *Brainwashing in Red China: The Calculated Destruction of Minds*. The Vanguard Press, Inc. (New York, 1951). "Brainwashing," pp. 3-18; "Learning," pp. 58-61.
Hunter describes the real life indoctrination process used in China in the 1950s. Note that physical force was not used. What is the difference between the philosophical indoctrination that you get at university, with its liberal/elitist/socio-economic slant, and that described in the book? How long would it take for you to breakdown and change your worldview?

Huxley, Aldous. *Brave New World Revisited*. Chatto & Windus (London, 1959). "Brainwashing," pp. 87-96.
Huxley describes the general threat of government sponsored reeducation efforts.

Zimbardo, Philip G., Ebbeson, Ebbe E. & Maslach, Christina. *Influencing Attitudes and Changing Behavior*, 2nd Ed. Addison-Wesley Publishing Company (Menlo Park, CA, 1977). "Posing Problems of Personal Influence," pp. 1-23.
This selection talks about the process of brainwashing in general and the case of Patty Hearst in particular. In the case of Patty Hearst, how different from her do you think that you are? Note that she changed her whole worldview and became a terrorist in less than two months with no physical force applied.

Plous, Scott. *The Psychology of Judgment and Decision Making*. Temple University Press (Philadelphia, 1993). Chapter 17—"Social Influences," pp. 191-204.

In this chapter, Plous documents how peer pressure and the views of those around us influence our behavior. How well do you think that you would fair in a modification of the "lines experiment"? What are the implications of this chapter with regard to people's values?

Pollock, John. *Contemporary Theories of Knowledge*. Rowman & Littlefield (Savage, MD, 1986). "A Brain in a Vat," pp. 1-4.

In this humorous article, Pollock illustrates that difficulty of knowing whether this world is real or just an illusion. What implications are there for your life, if the whole world is just an illusion?

Descartes, Rene. *Meditation and the First Philosophy*, Tweyman, Stanley, ed. Routledge (London, 1993). "Meditations I & II," pp. 45-57.

In his first Meditation, Descartes searches for an answer to the question, "How do I know that I am not deceived," even about the most basic things, such as the fact that he has five fingers. Follow his meditation. Concentrate and truly consider his question and follow his approach to an answer. Are you convinced, as Descartes was, that "I feel constrained to confess that there is nothing in the world that I formerly believed to be true, of which I cannot in some measure doubt…"? If you are convinced, what is the significance of the problem?

In his second Meditation, Descartes comes to realize that there is at least one thing of which he can have absolute clarity—"I am, I exist." From this single point, Descartes is then able to extrapolate a number of other things of which he can be certain. One such extrapolated point is the nature of the "I"—"a thing which thinks."

Bennett, Jonathan. "The Conscience of Huckleberry Finn." *Philosophy*, vol. 49, 1979, pp 123-143.

This article attempts to look at the inner workings of the minds of three people and how they justify their actions as moral. Each has developed a different concept of morality stemming from their own individual social, cultural, and religious background. The article shows how people rationalize their beliefs without investigating the legitimacy of their underlying foundation.

Cook, John W. *Morality and Cultural Relativism*. Oxford University Press (New York, 1999). Chapter 1—"Moral Relativism versus Moral Absolutism," pp. 7-12, and Chapter 2—"Moral Relativism: A Statement of the Doctrine," pp. 13-23.

Are you persuaded by the arguments in favor of moral relativism? Do you agree that because morality is a factor of socialization and cannot be learn by empirical-scientific study that moral principles cannot be "known"? It is impossible to know with certainty whether a moral position of yours is absolutely correct?

Bloom, Allan. *The Closing of the American Mind: How Higher Education Has Failed Democracy and Impoverished the Souls of Today's Students*. Simon and Schuster (New York, 1987). "Introduction: Our Virtue," pp. 25-43.

Bloom argues that the philosophy of relativism has led to a decline in critical thinking on the part of students and faculty in higher education, as well as to a lull in the drive to acquire knowledge. Is there truth to his indictment?

Kekes, John. *The Morality of Pluralism*. Princeton University Press (Princeton, 1993). "Introduction: Is our Morality Disintegrating," pp 3-8.
Kekes asserts that those who argue modern day morality is declining (such as Bloom of the previous reading) are in fact people trapped with "monistic" view of morality. Rather, he asserts there is no disintegration of value, but rather a shift in our society's "conception of morality," which is neither positive nor negative (albeit it is away from the conservative point of view expressed by its detractors). Do you agree with this assessment?

Kopelman, Loretta M. "Female Circumcision/Genital Mutilation and Ethical Relativism." Moser, Paul K. and Carson, Thomas L., eds. *Moral Relativism: A Reader.* Oxford University Press (New York, 2001). pp. 307-325.
Kopelman argues that absolute moral standards and judgment can be ascertained by assessing the justification offered by a society in support of a particular form of objectionable conduct. Do you agree? What would be the case if a society offered no justification for a particular offensive behavior, but rather merely asserted that it is a practice ordained by their religious faith (e.g. child sacrifice, pedophilia, female circumcision)?

Mivart, St. George. *On Truth: A Systematic Inquiry*. Kegan Paul, Trench & Co. (London, 1889). Chapter 1—"Evidence and Certainty," pp. 3-14.
Mivart argues that the existence of truth and certainty are self-evident: "Certainty exists, and universal doubt is unreasonable. There must be ultimate truths which do not need proof. The ground on which we believe them is their self-evidence, and no better criterion is possible."

Cook, John W. *Morality and Cultural Relativism*. Oxford University Press (New York, 1999). Chapter 1—"Moral Relativism versus Moral Absolutism," pp. 7-12, and Chapter 2—"Moral Relativism: A Statement of the Doctrine," pp. 13-23.
According the Cook, a cultural or moral relativist would object to the fact that truth can be obtained in the world of morality. The relativists would agree that truths about the physical world, scientific truths, can be known, but moral truths cannot, as they by their very natural subjective. Do you agree? Is the moral relativist's position inherently contradictory inasmuch they would enjoin a person from judging other cultures? Is this not an absolute moral position? Is there a way to know something other than by empirical study?

James, William. *Essay on Faith and Morals*. Longmans, Green and Co. (New York, 1949). "The Will to Believe," pp. 32-62.
This essay contains an interesting discussion of the relationship between knowledge and faith and their role in compelling action. James argues that some decisions, particularly moral decisions, cannot be made with absolute certainty. This creates a dilemma wherein a person must either act without sufficient evidence or not act for fear of being wrong. If James is correct, would it ever be morally justified to condemn the actions of another culture? Does he mean that we must at times make subjective, rather than objective, decisions on critical issues? How does James' position relate to the requirements of being an intellectual discussed in Chapter 4? Examine James' definition and application of a live option. He defines a live option as one which the individual actor would be willing to consider, regardless of its objective validity. Does this make sense to you?

Chisholm, Roderick M. *The Foundations of Knowing.* **Harvester Press (Sussex, 1982). "The Problem of The Criterion," pp. 61-75.**
In the beginning of this chapter, we introduced the philosophical question of how can we sure of anything and when is it that we can know anything. In truth, though, we did not answer this question directly. Rather, we pointed out that knowledge is attainable and to be sure there are things that we know. Now, however, that we are asking you to categorize your convictions and to indicate which ones are based on knowledge, we return to the original question more directly.

In this essay, Chisholm reiterates the classic problem defining something as being truly known. He identifies three approaches to its resolution: Skepticism, Empiricism, and what he calls "particularism." Which of these positions do you believe that this textbook supports? Does Chisholm's discussion help you in completing the exercise above of categorizing your convictions?

Wilson, John. *Language & the Pursuit of Truth.* **Cambridge University Press (Cambridge, 1956). Chapter III—"Truth," pp. 75-105.**
Discuss and critique this passage, evaluating what Wilson says about the "conditions for attaining truth" in relation to the ideas that he introduces into the discussion: intuition, conscience, emotion, faith.

index

Sponsors

In loving memory of Edward Shabot,
dedicated by his devoted wife and children

In loving memory Rachel Tawil, dedicated by her family

In loving memory of Elliot Chalme, dedicated by his family

In loving memory of Rabbi David Shamah

In loving memory of Joseph Harary, dedicated by his family

Adrienne and Steven Shalom Family
in memory of Seymour Shalom

In loving memory of Abe M. Cohen

In loving memory of Jaime and Mary Abadi

In loving memory of David and Milo Bibi

In honor of Charles and Brenda Saka

In honor of Danny and Shelley Massry

Mr. and Mrs. Albert Bijou

Mr. and Mrs. Ely Eddi

Mr. and Mrs. Michael J. Fallas

Mr. and Mrs. David E. Dweck

Mr. and Mrs. Eli D. Dweck

Mr. and Mrs. Eli M. Dweck

Mr. and Mrs. Morris Bailey

Mr. and Mrs. Joseph Jerome

Mr. and Mrs. Martin Salama

Mr. and Mrs. Joseph Chehebar

Mr. and Mrs. Jacob Deckelbaum

Mr. and Mrs. Jack Franco

Mr. and Mrs. Ronnie Shamah

Danny Yakoel and Haim Mizrahi